Okhrana

The Paris Operations of the Russian Imperial Police

Ben B. Fischer

History Staff
Center for the Study
of Intelligence

Central Intelligence Agency

1997

Foreword

Author/Compiler's Note: This is the first in a planned series of thematic collections of articles that appeared previously in classified editions of the Intelligence Community journal *Studies in Intelligence,* which is published at CIA. As part of its "openness" policy, CIA has declassified more than 1,200 articles from the first 40 years of *Studies.* We expect to compile and publish more collections of this type that address single intelligence-related themes or topics. We believe readers will find these articles interesting, informative, and colorful.

The author/compiler, Ben B. Fischer, would like to thank the following people for reading an earlier draft of the Preface, offering comments and criticisms, and identifying additional sources: Kay Oliver, Robert Pringle, James Bruce, David Thomas, and John Dziak. Thanks are also due to Elena Danielson and Carole Leadenham of the Hoover Institution at Stanford University for taking an interest in this project and supporting it. Rick Hernandez of Stanford University did a fine job with research assistance.

Contents

Preface

Okhrana: The Paris Operations of the Russian Imperial Police

by Ben B. Fischer

From Paris to Palo Alto

The first six articles reprinted below were published in *Studies in Intelligence* between 1965 and 1967. They describe foreign operations of the Russian Imperial Police, commonly referred to as the Okhrana, in the late 19th and early 20th centuries.[1] Also included are a letter from the author of these articles to *Studies in Intelligence* and the book review that prompted the letter, both of which discuss the still-debated issue of whether Josef Stalin was an Okhrana agent.

The 1883 opening of a Paris office known as the *Zagranichnaia okhranka* or *agentura*[2] was a sign of both success and failure on the part of the tsarist

---

[1] Russian contemporaries as well as present-day historians have used the term Okhrana to refer generically to the Ministry of Interior's Department of State Police, which was created in 1880 and renamed Department of Police in 1883. Strictly speaking, however, the term referred specifically to the security detail assigned to the tsar and the royal family.

The Department of Police included a unit known as the Special Section (*Osoby Otdel* or OO), which dealt with political crimes and sensitive investigations. The OO was a clandestine service, organizationally and physically separate from the regular police apparatus, but located on the fifth floor of the police headquarters at 16 Fontanka Quai, St. Petersburg. The OO formally commanded so-called *okhranoe otdelenie* or security sections from which the colloquial term Okhrana was derived, although in practice the subordinate units were more or less independent. (Full title: *otdelenie po okhraneniiu obshchestvennoi bezopastnosti i poriadka,* or section for maintaining public security and order.) The first three security sections were created in St. Petersburg, Moscow, and Warsaw. By 1911 there were 75 sections at the provincial, city, and oblast levels. See Ellis Tennant [pseudonym of Edward Ellis Smith], comp. and ed., "The Department of Police 1911-1913 from the Recollections of Nikolai Vladimirovich Veselago," in Edward Ellis Smith Collection, box 1, Hoover Institution Archives *passim*; Frederic S. Zuckerman, "Vladimir Burtsev and the Tsarist Political Police," *Journal of Contemporary History*, Vol. 12 (January 1977), p. 215n11 and *The Tsarist Secret Police in Russian Society, 1880-1917* (New York University Press, New York, 1996), p. xiv; George Leggett, *The Cheka: Lenin's Political Police* (New York: Oxford University Press, 1981), p. xxiii; Christopher Andrew and Oleg Gordievsky, *KGB: The Inside Story of Its Foreign Operations from Lenin to Gorbachev* (New York: Harper-Collins*Publishers*, 1990), pp. 20 ff; and Richard Pipes, *Russia Under the Old Regime* (New York: Collier Books/Macmillan Publishing Company, 1994), p. 301.

[2] The term Okhranka, which was sometimes used interchangeably with Okhrana, was frequently used to refer to the Paris office. The term *agentura* means agency or bureau, but it also referred to an agent network. *Zagranichnaia* means "foreign." See Edward Ellis Smith with Rudolf Lednicky, *"The Okhrana": The Russian Department of Police: A Bibliography* (Stanford, CA: The Hoover Institution on War, Revolution and Peace, 1967), p. 261. There were two foreign bureaus—the other one was in Bucharest—and both had satellite offices. The Paris office, for example, oversaw a subordinate unit in Berlin. Together the Paris and Bucharest offices ran all tsarist police and intelligence operations worldwide.

authorities. It reflected their success in having driven many revolutionaries, terrorists, and nationalists out of Russia; it also underscored their failure to stem an upsurge in Russian subversive activity based abroad. By the 1880s, the Russian emigre community in France had grown to some 5,000 people, most of them in the Paris area.[3] The City of Light had become the hub for Russian revolutionary groups operating in much of Europe.

The Okhrana's initial assumption—that exile in Europe rather than Siberia or some other remote place would act as a safety valve for such groups—proved erroneous. Russian emigrants did not assimilate quickly or easily, and some discovered that relatively greater freedom in the West gave them broad opportunities to engage in antiregime activities.

These essays portray not only the officials who ran the Okhrana's foreign bureau, but also the colorful agents, double agents, and *agents provocateurs* who worked for and against it—sometimes simultaneously. Many of these characters could have stepped out of the pages of a Conrad story or a le Carré novel, but their deeds were real and were recorded in the Paris office's files, which were hidden away for almost 30 years at the Hoover Institution on the campus of Stanford University.

The story of how these files made their way from Paris to Palo Alto is an intriguing tale. When Russian revolutionaries overthrew the 300-year-old Romanov dynasty in March 1917, they quickly turned their attention to their foes in the Okhrana. A multiparty committee was formed to investigate tsarist secret police offices and practices inside the Empire in St. Petersburg, Moscow, and Warsaw—as well as in Paris—with a view to prosecuting police officials of the ousted regime. The last imperial ambassador to France, Basil Maklakov, closed his mission in Paris and sealed its secret files, but he reopened them when the official inquiry began. After the short-lived Provisional Government fell to Lenin and the Bolsheviks in November 1917, Maklakov resealed the files and waited for further instructions.

France refused to resume relations with the radical new government in Moscow. It withheld recognition until 1924, when the USSR was formed.

---

[3] Ronald Hingley, *The Russian Secret Police: Muscovite, Imperial, and Soviet Political Security Operations* (New York: Simon & Schuster, 1970), p. 72.

Maklakov, meanwhile, was not idle. Taking advantage of the confusion in Moscow, he placed the Okhrana files in sixteen 500-pound packing crates, which were then bound with wire and sealed.

When the Bolsheviks finally got around to asking for "their" files in 1925, Maklakov—who had codenamed his concealment and removal operation "Tagil" after a Siberian village—swore he had burned them. The files, however, remained intact and were awaiting shipment to the Unites States. The ambassador convinced Christian Herter, then associated with Herbert Hoover's American Relief Administration and later Secretary of State under President Eisenhower, to help. Herter had a house in Paris, where the crates were stashed, and he later helped get them through French and US customs—with seals intact.[4]

It took two more years to arrange for the files to be moved from the eastern United States to California. Maklakov signed an agreement with the Hoover Institution stipulating that the crates would remain sealed until his death and would not be made public for another three months thereafter. The ex-ambassador no doubt feared retaliation from the Bolsheviks' dreaded intelligence service, the *Cheka,* which presumably would have sought to kill him if it had discovered what he had done with the Paris files.

Maklakov's contract with the Hoover Institution and his longevity—he died in Switzerland in 1957 at age 86—kept the archive under wraps for more than three decades. The Institution opened the packing crates at a gathering of reporters and photographers on 28 October 1957.[5] It took the privately supported Institution five more years to find funds and assemble a staff to organize and catalogue the files. A team headed by Dr. Andrew Kobal and under the supervision of Hoover assistant director Professor W.S. Sworakowski began working in June 1962 and finished in early 1964.[6] The archive attracted international scholarly interest, and *Life* magazine ran a feature story about it.

---

[4] Herter's role is being divulged here for the first time. In 1957 Herter was Acting Secretary of State, and the Hoover Institution thought it best not to reveal his role.
[5] Stanford University News Service, October 30, 1957 in Hoover Institution Records, box 179A; Archives Subject File A01, folder: Okhrana Project 1962.
See also "Czarist Dossiers on Reds Opened," *New York Times*, October 30, 1957, p. 10.
[6] Draft press release in Hoover Institution Records, box 179A, Archives Subject File A01, folder: Okhrana Project 1962.

Professor W.S. Sworakowski and an unidentified assistant at the Hoover Institution check unopened crates containing the Okhrana files in 1957. The shipping tag indicates that the crates were stored in Washington, DC, before being shipped to California. Courtesy of the Hoover Institution.

According to Hoover records, the archive contains 206 boxes, 26 scrapbooks, 164,000 cards, and eight linear feet of photographs. The complete archive is available on 509 reels of microfilm. It is a veritable who's who of the Russian revolution and includes files on and photographs of Stalin, Molotov, and Trotsky.

CIA Interest in the Okhrana Files

The author of the six articles, who used the pseudonym "Rita T. Kronenbitter," wrote them at the request of the CIA's Counterintelligence Staff. "Kronenbitter" was among the first researchers to display an interest in the Okhrana files. The articles originally were classified "confidential," presumably to avoid revelation of the CIA's interest in the Okhrana records.

Why was CIA counterintelligence interested in what the Hoover Institution's press release hailed as a "mother lode of knowledge on crucial years leading to the overthrow of the Romanovs in March 1917"? The Hoover archive was the only comprehensive collection of pre-1917 Russian police and intelligence files in the West. During the Soviet era, some specialists viewed these unique files as being of more than historical interest. British espionage historian Richard Deacon suggested why the Okhrana was of interest long after its demise when he wrote that the Russian police agency "was, in fact, a comprehensive, coordinated espionage and counterespionage organization, the most total form of espionage devised in the latter part of the 19th century *and still forming the basis of Soviet espionage and counterespionage today.*"[7] [emphasis added]

CIA's Counterintelligence Staff apparently believed these files would yield data on Russia's intelligence "culture" and methods that could provide new insights into Moscow's Soviet-era operations. Some at CIA challenged this notion, claiming that the KGB was a qualitatively new organization employing a different tradecraft.[8] Years later, former KGB officers Oleg Gordievsky and Oleg Kalugin asserted that the KGB had used Okhrana

---

[7] Richard Deacon, *A History of the Russian Secret Service* (London: Frederick Muller Ltd., 1972), p. 86.

[8] During James Jesus Angleton's tenure from 1954 to 1975, the CIA's Counterintelligence Staff regularly studied historical cases of Soviet intelligence operations, looking for insights into contemporary operations and methods. Critics complained that Angleton's staff wasted time and resources reexamining cases such as the *Trest* (Trust) deception operation of the 1920s and the *Rote Kapelle* (Red Orchestra) espionage network of the World War II era. They argued that the KGB—created in 1954—was an entirely new organization with new missions and tradecraft. See Tom Mangold, *Cold Warrior: James Jesus Angleton: The CIA's Master Spy Hunter* (New York: Simon & Schuster, 1991), pp. 60-61, 324-325, 330 *passim*. The same critics presumably would have been even more critical of studies of the pre-Soviet Okhrana. In fact, however, the historical literature on Russian and Soviet intelligence and counterintelligence is not particularly rich and in some cases is not reliable, so even "historical" studies were welcome to the counterintelligence specialists.

manuals in training and lecture courses when they were KGB trainees in the late 1950s and early 1960s. Kalugin claims that use of Okhrana materials continued into the 1980s.[9]

Origins of the Okhrana and Its Paris Office

The Okhrana was created in 1881 in response to the assassination of Alexander II. Its primary mission was to protect the tsar, the royal family, and the Russian autocracy itself.[10] Over time this evolved into an Empire-wide campaign against revolutionaries, terrorists, and assorted national minority groups seeking independence. Some revolutionaries wanted the tsar's head; others simply wanted to be free of his iron hand.

The opening in 1883 of the Okhrana's Foreign Bureau, centered in Paris, was prompted by the shift of Russian revolutionary activity from the Russian Empire to Western and Central Europe. The new Bureau occupied two modest offices in the Russian Imperial Consulate at 97 *Rue de Grenelle*. Never very large (see the first reprinted article below, entitled, "Paris Okhrana 1885-1905"), the Paris bureau nonetheless proved effective. It adopted and refined modern police and detective methods–as well as human intelligence agent operations–to achieve its objectives.[11]

The Okhrana saw Paris as the most advantageous place to base its foreign operations. Russian police officials admired the French internal security service, the *Sûreté Generale*—generally regarded as among the best in the world—and sought access to its files through both official liaison and unofficial channels. The Okhrana even hired French, British, and other detectives to help run its operations. From Paris, moreover, the Okhrana could monitor its *agenturas* in Berlin and other European cities. Most of the key

[9] See Andrew and Gordievsky, *KGB*, p. 22 and Oleg Kalugin, *Vid s Lubianki: "Delo" Byvshego Generala KGB* (Moscow: Nezavisimoe Izdatel'stvo, 1990), p. 35, as cited in Orlando Figes, *A People's Tragedy: A History of the Russian Revolution* (New York: Viking, 1996), p. 645n. In an English-language memoir, Oleg Kalugin notes that his training class read a detailed account of agent recruitment methods prepared by Nicholas II's chief of counterintelligence. See Oleg Kalugin with Fen Montaigne, *The First Directorate: My 32 Years in Intelligence and Counterintelligence Against the West* (New York: St. Martin's Press, 1994), p. 17.

[10] Creation of the Okhrana marked the emergence of the modern secret or political police apparatus. Its predecessor, the Third Section, was more in the tradition of a praetorian or palace guard aimed at thwarting plots and intrigues against the tsars by Russian aristocrats and nobles, especially at court and in the military. The Okhrana's main mission was dealing with the rise of the revolutionary intelligentsia in the latter part of the 19th century. See Richard J. Johnson, *"Zagranichnaia Agentura*: The Tsarist Political Police in Europe," in *Contemporary History*, Vol. 7 (January-April 1972), p. 222.

[11] There is no comprehensive history of the Okhrana's foreign operations. For a list of books and articles that describe its organization and methods, see Smith, "The Okhrana", pp. 65-67 and 230-242.

Russian revolutionaries in the French capital had contacts in other countries and cities. Consequently, penetrations of revolutionary groups in Paris often yielded leads to Russian dissident organizations and individuals outside France.

The Okhrana's relations with the *Sûreté* were symbiotic. The Okhrana reduced the *Sûreté's* workload and provided employment for retired French detectives. The French police did not see the Paris bureau as a threat to French national interests or to the *Sûreté's* organizational equities. On the eve of World War I the French security service declared: "It is impossible, on any objective assessment, to deny the usefulness of having a Russian police [force] operating in Paris, whether officially or not, whose presence is to keep under surveillance the activities of Russian revolutionaries."[12] At the same time, socialist and radical deputies in the French Assembly, who were more sympathetic to the Russian revolutionaries than to the police, pressed the French and Russian Governments to shut down the Okhrana office. In 1913 the Russian regime formally complied by announcing the office's closure. But this was a subterfuge; the Russian police continued operating under the cover of the *Agence Bint et Sambain*, a private detective agency. One of the two proprietors, Henri Bint, was a former employee of both the *Sûreté* and the Okhrana.[13]

Foreign Operations

The Foreign Bureau's operational methods evolved through three distinct phases. Initially, the Okhrana men believed they could keep tabs on Russian revolutionaries by hiring local surveillance teams and examining *Sûreté* files. This **"external" surveillance** (in Russian: *naruzhnoe nabludenie*) proved inadequate. French officials were reluctant to share their files, and French detectives hired by the Russians sometimes proved to be more loyal to their former employer (the *Sûreté*) than to their new paymaster. Even more important, French operatives could not penetrate the inner cores of Russian revolutionary and terrorist groups. Only Russian revolutionaries could.

In the second phase, the use of "internal" surveillance—**penetration** of subversive groups by recruiting agents from among their ranks or by sending in double agents—marked the Okhrana's transition from police methods to classic intelligence operations. (The Russians used the term *vnutrenniaia agentura*, or "internal agency," to refer collectively to the agents and double agents controlled by Okhrana units.)

[12] Cited in Andrew and Gordievsky, *KGB*, pp. 23-24.
[13] *Ibid.*, p. 24.

The Okhrana succeeded in penetrating many anti-tsarist organizations. It acquired agents throughout Russia and Europe. Some of these people spied because they were monarchists; others did so because they were romantic adventurers or simply mercenaries. The most interesting were the agents who began as real revolutionaries, were arrested, and then were "doubled" or "turned" by the Okhrana. Some responded to Okhrana blandishments because they feared jail or exile in Siberia—or worse—but for others it was simply a new career opportunity. Many who completed their undercover assignments "retired" and then were given good civilian jobs.

The third method of operation—the use of **agents provocateurs**—was the most controversial. The subject was so sensitive that the Okhrana officially denied it had run agents who organized and participated in sanctioned revolutionary acts. (This type of activity was the focus of the Provisional Government's 1917 inquiry into the Okhrana.)

In its 34-year existence, the Okhrana's Paris office had only four chiefs, giving it greater stability and continuity than its headquarters organization in St. Petersburg. As a result, the Paris bureau also enjoyed considerable autonomy in running its affairs, which included planning and executing operations, liaison with local and foreign police departments, agent recruitment and handling, and evaluation and reporting of information to the Okhrana's elite Special Section (see below).[14]

The Paris operatives developed rudimentary tradecraft for meeting and debriefing their agents—called *sekretnye sotrudniki* (secret collaborators) or *seksoti* for short—in safehouses. At its peak the Paris bureau had about 40 detectives on its payroll and some 30 agents in Paris and elsewhere in Europe. The Okhrana ran a major mail intercept program at home and abroad that yielded substantial information. Not for nothing was Russia known as the "gendarme of Europe." Between 1906 and 1914 the police succeeded in crushing popular opposition and penetrating—and in some cases even controlling—opposition political parties at home and abroad.[15] According to one historian, "virtually nothing that related to these parties

---

[14] Johnson, *"Zagranichaia Agentura,"* p. 226.
[15] D.C. B. Lieven, "The Security Police, Civil Rights, and the Fate of the Russian Empire, 1855-1917," in Olga Crisp and Linda Edmondson, eds., *Civil Rights in Imperial Russia* (Clarendon Press: Oxford, 1989), p. 246. Hingley claims that by 1909 the Okhrana had 150 agents inside the Socialist Revolutionary, Bolshevik, and Menshevik socialist parties and even in the less-threatening liberal Kadet party. Hingley, *The Russian Secret Police*, p. 100.

remained a secret from the government."[16] Key targets of surveillance and agent operations included:

- Émigré and revolutionary groups abroad.

- Revolutionaries arriving from Russia.

- Known centers of conspiratorial activity.

- Underground publishers and forgers (of passports, false identities, and so forth).

- Bomb-manufacturing "factories."

- Weapons and explosives smugglers.

- Russians with ties to European socialists and socialist organizations.

The Okhrana also provided VIP security for the royal family, other influential persons, and senior officials traveling abroad.[17]

The Okhrana's Special Section was an elite unit. It recruited exclusively from the Russian army. Successful candidates were assigned to the army's "Separate Corps of Gendarmes."[18] Prospective candidates were carefully screened and well trained. Tradecraft instruction included agent recruitment and agent handling; secret writing; "flaps and seals" (surreptitious reading of correspondence); reports writing; civil and criminal law; surveillance and investigative techniques; and the history of the Russian revolutionary movement. Assisting the officers were the *filiery*—detectives or surveillance men, most of whom were former army NCOs.[19]

The Okhrana also was capable of devastating blunders. The most notorious example was "Bloody Sunday" of 22 January 1905. When Father George Gapon, an Okhrana agent who had organized a police-sponsored workers' group, led a demonstration of peasants and workers to the Winter Palace in St. Petersburg, the *Gendarmerie,* without the tsar's authorization or advance knowledge, charged the crowd, killing or wounding at least 100 persons.

---

[16] Lieven, "The Security Police, Civil Rights, and the Fate of the Russian Empire, 1855-1917," p. 247.
[17] Johnson, "*Zagranichaia Agentura*," p. 232.
[18] Soldiers were considered reliable because they had sworn allegiance to the tsar.
[19] Tennant, "The Department of Police 1911-1913 from the Recollections of Nikolai Validimirovich Veselago," p. 18.

This was a seminal event in the eventual demise of the Romanov dynasty and Russian autocracy; it set in motion the first revolution of 1905 and ultimately led to the events of 1917.[20]

Change and Continuity

Examination of the Okhrana invites comparison with its Soviet successors from Lenin's *Cheka* to Stalin's NKVD to the KGB. There are common threads as well as important differences. The Okhrana, like the *Cheka*, was an internal security and counterintelligence agency *par excellence*. Its foreign operations were essentially an extension of its domestic security mission. The Soviet services before World War II focused heavily on actual and putative threats emanating from émigré groups, and well into the Cold War the KGB and its East European satellite services continued devoting considerable resources to the same target, even though they had other priorities.

The Okhrana pioneered many methods that the Soviet successor organs adapted and perfected. Systematic registration of politically suspect persons was accomplished in Moscow by the turn of the century and in St. Petersburg between 1906 and 1908.[21] Use of internal passports and mandatory registration of residences started with the Okhrana, not the Soviet intelligence and security agencies. The Okhrana—like its Soviet and Nazi counterparts—relied heavily on agents, co-optees, and busybodies in the general population to keep an eye on things. The organization of rural communities and urban apartment dwellers by city blocks was the same in Russia as in the Soviet Union—just more efficient in the latter.

In addition, the Okhrana—like the KGB, the *Gestapo*, and the East German *Stasi*—used its sources to monitor privately expressed views and popular moods and to prepare classified studies of latent popular attitudes that could

---

[20] As a result of Bloody Sunday, the tsar did not appear in public again until 1913, the tercentenary of the Romanov dynasty. In the months following the incident in St. Petersburg, the entire country, already suffering the strains of a losing war with Japan, experienced uprisings and revolts by workers, peasants, soldiers, and sailors. One result was the creation of the State Duma, which convened in 1906, but by and large political and social reforms were too little and too late. Even though Nicholas II did not authorize the police crackdown, Bloody Sunday helped destroy the centuries-old peasant image of the tsar as the godfather and savior of Russia. Gapon's demonstrators had gathered for the time-honored tradition of petitioning the tsar for relief from their manifold problems. See Figes, *A People's Tragedy*, pp. 3-15.

[21] Lieven, "The Security Police, Civil Rights, and the Fate of the Russian Empire, 1855-1917," p. 247.

not be freely voiced. The utilization of "black chambers" (an internationally used term that refers to facilities, often located in post offices, for mail and message interception, decoding, and decryption) began in Russia and reached its apogee in East Germany, where the *Stasi* read virtually all international correspondence and much of the domestic variety.

But the differences between the Okhrana and the later organizations are striking. As one authority notes, "what seems clear it that an unbroken patrimony between tsarist repression and Soviet terror cannot be claimed."[22] While secret police organizations served under tsars and commissars alike as the state security apparatus of the executive branch—and of the personal will of the Russian leader of the time—in the tsarist era there were substantial legal, political, and even ethical constraints. The Okhrana could order summary executions by hanging or firing squad, but only in extraordinary situations such as peasant uprisings and then only after Moscow had declared martial law. Although the Okhrana could deport political prisoners to Siberia, these and other administrative decisions were subject to judicial review. During the reign of Aleksandr II (1855-81) some 4,000 people were detained and interrogated in connection with political crimes, but few were executed.[23] From the mid-1860s to the mid-1890s, in fact, only 44 executions took place in Russia, and all were prompted by assassinations or assassination attempts against members of the royal family or government officials.

By contrast, on the day after Lenin launched the Red Terror in September 1918, the *Cheka* executed 500 people.[24] During Stalin's rule, the murderous NKVD acted as judge, jury, and executioner. The Red Terror under Stalin became the Great Terror; between 1935 and 1941 some 10 million people disappeared into the Gulag and three million were executed.[25]

Richard Pipes noted three restraints on the Okhrana: private property, inefficiency, and the imperial political elite's desire to be seen as culturally "Western."[26] Under the Bolsheviks these restraints vanished.

The Okhrana never aspired to the territorial and economic empire and extensive military and paramilitary forces commanded by the NKVD. Even the KGB—supposedly a kinder, gentler version of the NKVD operating under "socialist legality"—was more ruthless than its Russian antecedent. A comparison of Aleksandr III's treatment of Leo Tolstoy and Brezhnev's

[22] John J. Dziak, *Chekisty: A History of the KGB* (Lexington, MA: Lexington Books/D.C. Heath and Company, 1988), p. 31.
[23] Pipes, *Russia under the Old Regime*, p. 315.
[24] *Ibid.*, p. 317.
[25] John Channon with Rob Hudson, *The Penguin Atlas of Russia* (London: Penguin, 1995), p. 113.
[26] Pipes, *Russia under the Old Regime*, p. 312.

handling of dissidents such as Aleksandr Solzhenitsyn illustrates the point. Novelist Tolstoy was the best-known dissident of his day, and the police kept him under surveillance and censored his work. But they did not imprison him or prevent him from traveling and publishing abroad. During Stalin's reign, by contrast, Solzhenitsyn, like other dissidents, simply disappeared into the harsh internal exile system that he later dubbed the Gulag Archipelago. Even under Stalin's successors, intellectuals and political activists who dissented—including Solzhenitsyn and Andrei Sakharov— were subjected to inhumane treatment considered unacceptable by Western standards.[27]

Although the Okhrana was not as ruthless as the *Cheka* or the NKVD, in an ironic way it inspired them. Lenin and Stalin seemed to have concluded from their underground years that the tsarist police were too lenient.[28] After all, for all its success until 1914, the Okhrana had not been able to prevent a small group of radicals from seizing power three years later.

The Bolsheviks also learned how easy it had been for the Okhrana to plant agents within their inner circle. Dr. Jacob Zhitomirsky was a leading Bolshevik and Lenin confidant before he was discovered.[29] An even more dramatic example was the tsarist agent Roman Malinovsky—leader of the Bolshevik deputies in the fourth state *Duma*, a central committee member, and Lenin's chief lieutenant while the latter was still in exile.[30] When Vladimir Burtsev finally convinced Lenin that Zhitomirsky might be a double agent, the Bolshevik leader ordered Malinovsky to conduct an investigation.[31] Such experiences were, perhaps, at the root of Bolshevik paranoia—the urge to see enemies everywhere and eliminate them—that reached its bloody apogee under Stalin.

[27] During the late 1960s and 1970s the Soviet politburo and the KGB, led by Yuri Andropov, waged a campaign of terror, repression, and disinformation against Solzhenitsyn. One example: the KGB detained and so brutally interrogated one of the author's typists, Elizaveta Voronyan-skaya, that she broke down and divulged where a copy of *The Gulag Archipelago* was hidden. In despair, she committed suicide. She was secretly buried to cover up the KGB's crime. Dozens of official documents on the anti-Solzhenitsyn campaign were translated and edited in Michael Scammell, ed., *The Solzhenitsyn Files: Secret Soviet Documents Reveal One Man's Fight Against the Monolith* (Chicago: edition q, inc., 1995).

[28] Figes argues that the Okhrana's mistreatment of imprisoned revolutionaries brutalized them and whetted their appetite for revenge once the political tables were turned. "One can draw a straight line from the penal rigors of the tsarist regime to the terrorism of the revolutionaries and indeed to the police state of the Bolsheviks." *A People's Tragedy*, p. 124. There may be some truth to this, but the Bolsheviks, in quickly creating a police apparatus of their own, seemed motivated more by a desire to maintain power than by any quest for revenge against their former tormentors.

[29] Historian Bertram D. Wolfe claims that Harting and Zhitomirsky were one and the same, but the latter was actually the former's agent. Bertram D. Wolfe, *Three Who Made a Revolution: A Biographical History* (Boston: Beacon Hill Press, 1955), p. 536.

[30] Ibid., pp 535-557

[31] Dziak, *Chekisty*, p. 5.

The Okhrana's penetration of the Bolshevik party was so extensive and so thorough that the police files constitute the most complete (and only reliable) record of the conspiratorial party's early history, internal organization, membership, and deliberations—an unintentional contribution to future historians.[32] This was not the only unintended consequence. By penetrating the radical groups, the tsarist police were using a classic divide-and-conquer tactic to prevent formation of a unified opposition. Ironically, this tactic was most successful in preventing the emergence of an open opposition party with a mass base, and thus it helped to create an environment in which Lenin's small monolithic party of professional revolutionaries could flourish.

The Okhrana targeted liberals and revolutionaries alike, seeing both groups as threats to the Russian autocracy. But the two groups drew different lessons from their persecution at the hands of the tsarist police. When the Provisional Government came to power, it convened a special commission to investigate the organization, operations, and methods of the tsarist police—not to emulate them, but to correct past abuses and prevent their repetition.[33] Lenin and the Bolsheviks also studied the Okhrana, and so did KGB recruits decades later, to learn from and improve on the tsarist police's repressive methods.

Dramatis Personae

Agent provocateur is a French term, but the Russians perfected the art. In fact, the primary purpose of the Foreign Bureau's provocations was to scare the French into taking action against Russian radicals and cooperating with the Okhrana. The most notorious provocation occurred in Paris in 1890, when Arkadiy Harting (a.k.a. Abraham Gekel'man or Landezen) organized a well-armed team of bombthrowers and then betrayed them to the Paris police. These heavily publicized arrests helped persuade the French public of the dangers posed by Russian revolutionaries in France. The episode also convinced officials in St. Petersburg that republican France could get tough on Russian radicals and make a good ally. To some extent, at least, this helped diminish mutual suspicions and created an atmosphere on both sides conducive to negotiation of the Franco-Russian alliance of 1891.

---

[32] Leggett writes: "The extent of the Okhrana's penetration of the Bolshevik Party was such that not only was it minutely informed about the membership, structure, and activities of the party (one of the best sources of the pre-1917 Bolshevik Party history is a collection of Moscow Okhrana documents), but it was also in a position to influence Bolshevik tactics." (*The Cheka*, p. xxiv.)

[33] Tennant, "The Department of Police 1911 - 1913 from "Recollections of Nikolai Vladimirovich Veselago," p. 8.

Vladimir Burtsev, leading counterespionage specialist in the Russian revolutionary opposition to the tsarist government. Courtesy of the Hoover Institution.

Harting may be the most interesting character in the essays (see the second reprinted article below, entitled "The Illustrious Career of Arkadiy Harting"). He rose from informer to master spy to spymaster, eventually becoming chief of the Paris office. As noted above, his top agent, Zhitomirsky, penetrated Lenin's inner circle during the Bolshevik party's underground days. Before he quit the espionage business in 1909 following his exposure by the French press as a Russian spy, Harting had served tsarist Russia, imperial Germany, and republican France, receiving decorations from all three.

Harting met his match in Vladimir Burtsev (see the third reprinted article, entitled "The Sherlock Holmes of the Revolution"). Burtsev was a revolutionary by profession but a counterespionage expert by talent. He organized what in effect was a highly professional counterespionage bureau for Russian radicals. In 1909 Burtsev personally unmasked a major Okhrana agent, Evno Azef. Also in 1909, after years of relentless effort, Burtsev succeeded in proving that a terrorist known as "Landesen", who had escaped from the French police in 1890, actually was Harting. This was leaked to the press, prompting Harting to flee to Brussels, where he went into hiding and was never heard from again.[34]

Harting's case officer was Pyotr Rachkovsky, probably the ablest head of the Okhrana's Foreign Bureau. Rachkovsky was a pioneer. He refined the art of what we today call active measures or perceptions management techniques. He paid subsidies to journalists willing to write articles favorable to Russian interests, and he purchased or subsidized such periodicals as *Revue Russe* and *Le Courier Franco-Russe*. During his tenure (1884-1902), journalists on the Okhrana payroll began planting articles in the French press that were favorable to Russian interests. Rachkovsky also created the *Ligue pour le Salut de la Patrie Russe*, which promoted positive views toward Russia among French citizens; this group was a forerunner of Soviet front organizations and "friendship societies."

According to one authority, Rachkovsky was a "born intriguer" who "delighted" in forging documents. He allegedly was among those responsible for the anti-Semitic *Protocols of the Elders of Zion*, perhaps the most infamous political forgery of the 20th century.[35] Rachkovsky's tactic of exploiting anti-Semitism for political purposes was used repeatedly during the Soviet era—for example, in Hungary in 1956, in Czechoslovakia in 1968, and in Poland in the 1980s. Such scapegoating also was evident in the so-called "Doctors Plot" in the early 1950s, when a group of Jewish doctors was accused of plotting to kill Stalin and other Soviet leaders.

Rachkovsky was a model for subsequent Soviet practice in another regard. He was an advocate of Franco-Russian rapprochement and served as the tsar's personal emissary in secret negotiations leading to the Dual Alliance of 1891-94 and its modification in 1899.

---

[34] For more on Burtsev's exploits against the Okhrana, which for a time almost leveled the playing field for the revolutionaries, see Zuckerman, "Vladimir Burtsev and the Tsarist Political Police," pp. 193-219.

[35] Norman Cohn, *Warrant for Genocide: The Myth of the Jewish World Conspiracy and the Protocols of the Elders of Zion* (New York: Harper and Row, 1967), pp. 80-81.

The practice of using foreign intelligence officers on sensitive international assignments, bypassing the foreign ministry and regular diplomatic channels, was a standard Soviet modus operandi. Stalin used his head of foreign intelligence, Vladimir Dekanozov, to set the stage for his pre-World War II alliance with Hitler. Later, Khrushchev relied on a KGB officer under journalistic cover to establish a direct link to the Kennedy White House. After this emissary discredited himself by lying to the Kennedy brothers about the presence of Soviet missiles in Cuba, Khrushchev turned to the KGB resident to open another channel to the White House through ABC newsman John Scali; proposals that were floated through this channel eventually resolved the October 1962 missile crisis. In 1969 Brezhnev and Andropov assigned two senior KGB German experts to open a back channel to the new Social Democratic–led coalition government in Bonn.[36] The result was secret negotiation of a series of bilateral and multilateral agreements that transformed Soviet relations with West Germany and the rest of Europe.

Ventsion Moiseev-Moshkov Dolin was a classic double agent. (Running double agents has long been a quintessentially Russian skill, practiced before, during, and after the Soviet period.) Dolin began his career as an Okhrana penetration of anarcho-communist groups (see the fourth reprinted article, "Okhrana Agent Dolin"). On the eve of World War I he began working for German military intelligence—or so the Germans thought. He was in fact a double agent who had remained loyal to Russia. With help from the Okhrana, Dolin organized "successful" sabotage operations inside Russian weapons and munitions factories—operations that were "documented" in press articles.

The Germans were so pleased with Dolin that they asked him to conduct psychological warfare operations aimed at stirring up Russian workers to overthrow the monarchy and take Russia out of the war. "Kronenbitter" neglects to mention that when Dolin's efforts fell short of expectations, the Germans turned to another Russian agent on their payroll by the name of Vladimir Lenin. He was more successful, and the rest, as they say, is history.

The Okhrana was, in a limited sense, ahead of its time as an equal opportunity employer. It recruited people of all nationalities–and especially

[36] See Vyacheslav Kevorkov, *The Secret Channel: Moscow, the KGB and Bonn's Eastern Policy* [in German] (Berlin: Rowohlt, 1995).

women–as agents.[37] Women, in fact, were crucial to its operations and were paid as well or better than their male counterparts (see the fifth and sixth reprinted articles—"The Okhrana's Female Agents," Parts I and II). Women, however, were not permitted to become staff officers or managers–only agents.

The women were at least as colorful as the men—maybe more so. One example was "Francesco," the wife of a respected Moscow physician. While a student at Moscow University, she made three vows: to love her husband, to help kill the tsar, and to work for the Okhrana. Only the last promise was kept.

Another interesting female operative was known only as *La Petite*. As a 13-year-old milkmaid, she spied for Polish nationalists while delivering milk to the Okhrana office in Warsaw. Her target: office trash cans that sometimes contained copies of secret messages and names of informants in Poland. During World War I she worked for the Russians against the Austro-Hungarian Empire, posing as an Austrian citizen. After the war she retired to Monte Carlo, where she was known as *L'Autrichienne*.

Conclusions

The Kronenbitter collection reveals the Okhrana's foreign operations through anecdote, not analysis. The articles are entertaining and yet still

[37] Anna Geifman notes that as the turn of the century approached, women, especially those from upper- and middle-class backgrounds, became involved in underground politics and even in extremist acts: "As a result of rapidly changing family relations and the spread of literacy, self-assertive girls and young women could no longer be confined to the home. At the same time, however, they were denied higher education, along with any role in the political process, and in general were offered little opportunity to realize their intellectual ambitions. This drove a number of them into the ranks of the radical outcasts, where their male comrades were willing to give them greater recognition than could reasonably be expected within the traditional establishment. . . .To a large extent, this accounts for the fact that women comprised nearly one-third of the SR [Socialist Revolutionary] Combat Organization, and *approximately one-fourth of all Russian terrorists at the beginning of the century.*" [emphasis added] Anna Geifman, *Thou Shalt Kill: Revolutionary Terrorism in Russia, 1894-1917* (Princeton: Princeton University Press, 1996), p. 12. This involvement also made women natural targets of police surveillance and recruitment.

inform in a loosely structured way. For historians they suggest possibilities for more in-depth studies of Russian intelligence and counterintelligence operations in their formative period.[38] For observers of the contemporary scene they give insight into the apparent paradox of the "new" Russia, which, recent events have demonstrated, still gives high priority to foreign intelligence and counterintelligence operations.

The Soviet Union and the Communist Party and even the KGB are gone, but Russia "retains a strong intelligence profile and a traditional intelligence culture that are distinct from and even alien to our own."[39] Major-power espionage and counterespionage today have a less ideological rationale than during the Cold War, but the Russians do set forth a justification, couched in terms of vital national interests and security. The Okhrana story illustrates what history, even narrative history that is not primarily analytical, can offer—namely, events and insights from the past that have implications for the present and the future.

---

[38] For an example of solid scholarship based in part on the Okhrana Collection at the Hoover Institution, see Geifman's book cited in the previous footnote.
[39] James Sherr, "Cultures of Spying," *The National Interest*, No. 38 (Winter 1994/95), p. 60.

The views expressed in this Preface are those of the author. They do not necessarily reflect the views of the Central Intelligence Agency or any other US Government entity.

S-46

APPROVED FOR RELEASE
CIA HISTORICAL REVIEW PROGRAM
22 SEPT 93

~~CONFIDENTIAL~~

The larva and pupa stages, as it were, of the Tsarist political police's main center for anti-revolutionary work abroad.

PARIS OKHRANA 1885-1905 [1]

Rita T. Kronenbitter

The numerical strength of the Okhrana at home and abroad has been subject to much exaggeration. According to some Communist versions published both before and after the revolution, tens of thousands of Okhrana officials and agents in mufti were placed in every province of the Empire to prey upon the peaceful people and brutalize them. The agency is pictured as running a police state within the autocracy, subject to no authority and exerting its power on all, from the Tsar and his court down to the remotest muzhiks. The Okhrana's own documents show that this picture is largely propaganda.

In consideration of the size and population of the Empire and the tasks that faced the Okhrana, it seems about the smallest government agency in Russia, in most of the gubernias quite insignificant. According to Aleksei Vassiliev, the last director of police under the Tsar, it never had in all of Russia more than a thousand men.[2] Headquarters in Petrograd had fewer than 200 employees in all sections; Moscow's office was much smaller; and the branches at the seats of gubernias and volosts normally had two or three employees each.

The Okhrana abroad was likewise surprisingly small, and its requirements for headquarters support engaged less manpower than one would expect of a fairly modern and very active system. Agents under the Paris center employed in penetration operations had to be backstopped by headquarters or branch offices within the Empire

---

[1] Based chiefly on its files in the collection *Zagranichnaya Okhrana* recently opened to the public at the Hoover Institution. For earlier articles from this source see "The Okhrana's Female Agents," Parts I and II, in *Studies* IX 2, p. 25 ff and IX 3, p. 59 ff, and "Okhrana Agent Dolin," *Studies* X 2, p. 57 ff.

[2] A. T. Vassiliev, *The Okhrana* (London), p. 38.

with legends, documents, money, and whatever else was required to make their positions safe and tenable among the revolutionaries. It seems clear that headquarters and Paris must both have been practical, imaginative, and expeditious to meet such exacting demands with an extremely small number of personnel.

Cumulatively, the total number employed by the Paris center from its beginnings under Rachkovsky in 1885 to March 1917 when the revolution terminated it was almost one thousand. This includes everyone who received remuneration for services rendered in any capacity during the 32 years—chiefs, assistants, office administrators, staff agents under deep cover for penetration operations, Russian penetration agents and correspondents, non-Russian principal agents supervising investigation and surveillance networks, the hired detectives under their supervision or working independently, informers and police officials paid for their cooperation.

The operations were in perpetual flux. Many officers and agents served for long periods, but their duties were subject to constant change. Only the chief and his office staff, seldom numbering more than eight people, were a stable group. Some two hundred internal (penetration) and external (detective) agents operating at the height of the center's activities were subject to the most diverse movements and assignments. The networks formed and reformed for tasks in Germany, France, Italy, and elsewhere.

The Paris center had a somewhat different character under each of its four successive chiefs. While the paramount task of each was the same—collecting intelligence on revolutionary movements—it happened that each was confronted with a new situation requiring revision of plans and concentration of effort in new directions. Each also had his own style of operation. Not counting an abortive effort begun by Korvin-Krukovskoi in June 1883 which ended in January 1885 with his dismissal, the successive administrations were as follows:

Peter Ivanovich Rachkovsky—March 1885 to November 1902
Leonid Aleksandrovich Rataev—November 1902 to August 1905
Arkady Mikhailovich Harting—August 1905 to January 1909
Acting: Captain Andreev and Captain Dolgov—February to November 1909
Aleksandr Aleksandrovich Krassilnikov—November 1909 to March 1919

This article will examine the first two of them.

Paris Okhrana ~~CONFIDENTIAL~~

Rachkovsky: Office and External Nets

Arriving in Paris in March 1885, Rachkovsky found no records covering Korvin-Krukovskoi's nearly two years of service; there was not even an office for him to take over. The only organized remnant was a group of detectives under an ex-Sûreté agent named Barlet. Krukovskoi had been paying this "Barlet Brigade" mostly for reports copied down in the French police and security offices; its members did not conduct any surveillance and investigations for themselves. At best the Brigade amounted to a liaison arrangement exploiting personal connections in various French offices.

Rachkovsky was given two rooms in a side wing of the Imperial Embassy at 97 rue de Grenelle, with a separate entrance from the courtyard. He installed an additional door with a lock in the hall and heavy bars in the windows. His T/O called for three assistants, to be selected from among MVD personnel already in France and Switzerland. He chose Leonty Golshman, a long-time MVD correspondent, and for clerical and code work Nikolai Chashnikov, an embassy employee fluent in French. Throughout his tenure, until 1902, these two remained his only permanent office staff.

Okhrana chief Semiakin, in his earlier capacity as a sort of inspector general, had found the Barlet Brigade the one thing he could praise in Krukovskoi's operation; but Rachkovsky was never quite happy with it. On headquarters' insistence he renewed the contract and increased the number of agents to six. But he soon realized that he could not buy their primary loyalty away from their former employer, the Sûreté. He needed completely independent investigators to go beyond what Brigade members could get from the daily transcripts in police and security offices; the host services would make available only what it was in their interest to pass on to the Russians. He was anxious also to learn as much as possible about the French services themselves, especially about their principal leaders. Before terminating the contract with Barlet in 1887, therefore, he cultivated agent Riant, one of the Brigade, to the point that he supplied information on the Sûreté and its leaders.

Under the terms of the contract Barlet maintained a private office to which the members of the Brigade brought their reports for transmission to Rachkovsky. Safe quarters were used for all communication, and the usual contact was Rachkovsky's assistant Golshman. None of the Brigade had access to the offices at 97 rue de Grenelle. When the contract was terminated, Rachkovsky assigned a formerly

1. *(Continued)*

independent MVD agent, Wladislaw Milewski, to serve as case officer for all external, non-Russian agents. Milewski rented a new safe house, got in touch with former Brigade members Riant and Bint, and rehired them and two new men, Douget and Dove. An experienced anti-revolutionary operator in Paris and London, he trained the four in surveillance to supplement the liaison work with the French services.

As soon as his safe house was ready for business and the new team was reporting to it, Milewski made a trip to London and hired two external agents there. One was a certain Murphy, a long-time acquaintance of his in Scotland Yard; the other he called "John." He gave both of them instructions to report directly to his address in Paris on the activities of Russian revolutionaries in England. The information was to be obtained from contacts in Scotland Yard and from their own observation. This was an informal beginning of the London outpost of Paris Okhrana.

Penetration Agents

Some half dozen agents sent abroad by the MVD were already in circulation in France and Switzerland, reporting directly to headquarters by personal correspondence or through consular channels. But none was fulfilling the requirement for inside information on revolutionary activities, and it was Rachkovsky's principal mission to organize penetrations of the adversary. Impatient for the formation of at least a small group of internal agents for such penetrations, headquarters had sent to France and Switzerland an MVD counsellor, S. Zvoliansky, to smooth the way for the Paris center and to spot recruits. After reviewing Rachkovsky's initial efforts, Zvoliansky now urged headquarters not to pester him for immediate reports but to give him time to organize the internal service. He asked also that Rachkovsky be sent to Switzerland to study the targets there and locate possible recruits.

The first such recruit was found in Zurich. He was studying at the Polytechnical College under the name Landesen, in hiding from the revolutionaries. Under his true name, Abraham Hackelman, he had been exposed as a police agent working among students belonging to the terrorist Narodnaia Volia at Petersburg and Riga. But headquarters' evaluation of him was most complimentary and he was recommended for rehiring. Rachkovsky agreed to pay him a monthly salary of 300 rubles plus travel expenses. His targets would

1. *(Continued)*

be the Narodnaia Volia exiles and newly formed groups of the Socialist Revolutionaries.

Other recruitments followed slowly. By the end of 1885, Rachkovsky had three penetration agents—Landesen among the Narodnaia Volia terrorists in Paris and Switzerland, Ignaty Kornfeld among the Anarcho-Communists, and Prodeus, a much traveled and well-known revolutionary, reporting on various revolutionary centers. Rachkovsky clearly recognized that his main task was to penetrate the conspiratorial groups, but he proceeded with extreme caution in building up the organization to do the job. Incoming dispatches brought many nominations from headquarters, but he ruled most of them out for lack of access to target groups or other reasons.

It was probably because of this cautious pace in Paris that Okhrana headquarters and the branches in Moscow, Odessa, Kiev, and elsewhere sent other agents abroad on penetration assignment with instructions to report directly home. The practice led to much confusion. The Paris office did not know when Odessa, Kiev, or Moscow had an agent in France, Switzerland, or England. Moreover, Okhrana headquarters itself was not always informed when a local branch sent an agent abroad. Despite much correspondence in the matter, it was only Rachkovsky's successors that succeeded in getting agent operations abroad coordinated. As the system worked during his term in Paris, he had no knowledge of such agents as the famous Evno Azev working under headquarters control in Germany and Switzerland.

During the Rachkovsky period the Paris internal service came to include the following major penetration agents:

Ilya Drezhner among the Social Democrats in Germany, Switzerland, and France;
Boleslaw Malankiewicz among the Polish anarchists and terrorists in London;
Casimir Pilenas, a spotter for Scotland Yard recruited to work among the Latvian terrorists;
Zinaida Zhuchenko among the Socialist Revolutionaries and their terrorist Fighting Unit;[3]
Aleksandr Evalenko, assigned by headquarters to New York City for work among the Jewish Bundists and terrorists, but under Paris control.

---

[3] For her story see the "Francesco" case in *Studies* IX 2, p. 28 ff.

23

1. *(Continued)*

Modus Operandi

No system of case officers or intermediaries between the Paris chief and the penetration agents was really established under Rachkovsky or his immediate successor, Rataev. When in Paris, these agents would report directly to Rachkovsky or sometimes to his case officer for the external service, Milewski. From elsewhere they reported either by mail or through confidants in the Russian consulates, as Evalenko did from New York.

The Paris office enjoyed an ambiguous relationship with autonomous agenturas in Berlin and Sofia. Rachkovsky had founded the one in Berlin, but a headquarters memorandum of 9 December 1900 gave it an independent chief, Arkady Harting, who was the same Abraham Hackelman that Rachkovsky had recruited under the name Landesen as his first penetration agent fifteen years before. Berlin like Paris had an internal and an external service, each set of agents reporting to a different case officer in a safe house. The case officer for the external agents, principal among them Carl Woltz and Henry Neuhaus, was Michael Barkov. For the internal agents Harting himself, like Rachkovsky, often had to serve as case officer; headquarters was still reluctant to assign permanent staff personnel to such duties. In 1902 Harting acquired the important penetration agent Dr. Jacob Zhitomirsky, who worked among the Social Democrats in close association with Lenin and Litvinov.

The Balkan agentura came under Rachkovsky's control by default. A service had operated there since the early 1880's as an outpost of the Odessa Branch. It followed the activities of subversives in Rumania and along the Bessarabian border. Because of inadequate headquarters control of this—as of other operations abroad—the expanding efforts required in the Balkan countries were integrated under general supervision from Paris. A Colonel Trzhestyak headed this Sofia service, with case officer Ivan Osadchuck handling the agents.

Under Rachkovsky's direction the Okhrana abroad was thus not a well constituted and integrated intelligence service. Shortage of personnel made necessary a constant shifting of agents in order to obtain some coverage of the multiplying centers of Russian subversives in Western Europe. There was no adequate control of operations through experienced case officers; agents had to be left to their own devices to run themselves.

60

1. *(Continued)*

Rachkovsky as Diplomat

By personally winning the good will and cooperation of the services of host countries, however, Rachkovsky indirectly assisted his agents and crowned their efforts. For instance, when a penetration agent in Geneva had supplied the essential information about a gathering of terrorists there and external agents had located by surveillance their clandestine printshop and weapons store, Rachkovsky could call on Swiss security units to help destroy the underground and arrest the ringleaders. This happened in 1887; it was repeated in 1888, then again and again in other countries. His powers of persuasion were sufficient to convert Lev Tikhomirov, one of the leading terrorists, when he had been softened by contrived exposure, and get him to write an anti-revolutionary book.

Rachkovsky's political action operations, often highly successful, were exclusively his personal effort. He devised some plans for using others, but in every major instance he was the sole operator. He befriended a Danish journalist, Jules Hansen, during his first visit to Paris in 1884. Besides being one of the bright lights of his profession, Hansen was a counsellor in the French Ministry of Foreign Affairs and a friend of Minister Delcassé. He became the principal channel for promoting a friendly press for Russia in western Europe, and he made contacts for Rachkovsky with leading ministers and politicians, including even President Loubet. On the other hand, Rachkovsky also cultivated important personages in the imperial government and at court. In these activities he was, as revolutionary writers accused him of being, a manipulator behind the scenes preparing the ground for acceptance, both in Paris and at Petersburg, of the Franco-Russian alliance signed in 1893.

Rachkovsky devised and developed access to several other governments beside the French. The files contain copies of dispatches about an audience he had with Pope Leo XIII and a proposed exchange of diplomats between Russia and the Vatican with particular view to the unrest in Catholic Poland. Advisers to the Tsar in Petersburg turned down the proposal, but the idea of combatting the insurrectional campaign in Poland by using religious interests clearly illustrates Rachkovsky's high-level concept of political action.

Rachkovsky's major provocation operation—his were probably the only specifically planned instances of this formally banned practice in the annals of Okhrana—was primarily in support of political action. In 1890 agent Landesen, having promoted among the revolutionaries in Paris an elaborate plot to kill the Tsar, arranged that after one underground meeting a large number of the terrorists would each have on their persons their weapons and written notes on the parts they were to play. The French police, tipped off through cutouts by Rachkovsky, arrested the entire group, and that summer they were tried and sentenced, Landesen in absentia. Rachkovsky thus scored a victory not only over the enemies of the state but against those in Petersburg who had opposed the Franco-Russian alliance on the grounds that France was too soft on subversives. The stern police and court action proved to Petersburg that France too had a strong government capable of dealing with internal enemies.

Despite his many successes in this formative age of Paris Okhrana, Rachkovsky was dismissed in 1902, principally because he dared expose in an intelligence report a charlatan and hypnotist named Philippe who told fortunes for the imperial household. His enemies at headquarters used this report to turn Tsar Nicolas against him. In 1905, however, after martial law was introduced at Petersburg, he was brought back to head the entire Okhrana, first as MVD Special Commissioner and then as Deputy Director of Police.

Rataev: Decline

In 1902 the annual authorized expenditures of Paris Okhrana were about 267,000 francs. This amount did not include the cost of agents sent from headquarters and provincial branches to operate abroad independently of the Paris office, and it did not cover the funding of the Balkan and Berlin agenturas. It covered the costs of the Paris office and safe houses, the salaries of external and internal agents and their case officers, and the needs of outposts in Switzerland, England, and Galicia.

Director of Police Lopukhin, who had never been friendly toward Rachkovsky, favored the selection of Leonid Rataev for the Paris post and increased the personal allowance for it with his appointment. But he also instructed the new chief to cut off the salaries of all agents not reporting directly to him. Rataev was apparently ill qualified for the Paris post, as he had been for his prior job as personnel chief of the Petersburg Okhrana. He had been in police service for some twenty years, but both of his bosses, the Director of Police and the MVD Minister, considered him a weak administrator, little more than a socialite figurehead, and regarded his appointment to Paris as a way to get rid of an incompetent at headquarters. At the same time they anticipated that he would be easier to handle there from headquarters than the vigorous, independent, and scheming Rachkovsky.

Rataev proved to be as ineffective a manager as they expected. Although the number of penetration agents under him increased, none of these were his recruits. They were sent abroad by headquarters and such branches as Moscow, Kiev, and Warsaw; after reporting at first to their original offices, they were transferred to Paris for administrative and operational handling. Rataev did nothing, either, to develop professional case officers but let his office staff manage all agent personnel.

A contraction of Rataev's mission began to be noticeable soon after his arrival. His budget total was lowered step by step until it was halved at 135,000 francs. The Galicia outpost was taken away from Paris control, first being made an autonomous unit and then put under Warsaw Branch. Harting in the Berlin agentura, a friend of Rachkovsky, was *ergo* an enemy of Rataev, and Berlin very soon began to encroach on areas in the Paris domain—Switzerland, Austria, the Low Countries. Rataev protested, but to no apparent effect.

Penetrations

What made Rataev as successful as he was in collecting intelligence and disarming the revolutionaries was a small group of the Okhrana's ace agents assigned to the Paris center. These men and women came fully briefed from headquarters, impressively backstopped in Russia, and with their operational targets fully spelled out. Rataev's office was thus little more than a support facility for them, paying salaries and expenses and handling communications. Agents' reports, to be sure, were prepared as outgoing dispatches by Golshman, who had become an excellent editor, but Rataev contributed very little to mounting operations and handling the agents.

The first team of three agents assigned to Paris by headquarters was headed by Leo Beitner; the other two members were his wife and his unmarried sister Maria. They were to operate in Paris, Geneva, and Brussels. In Paris, Leo's target was the home of Vladimir Burtzev, which served as a revolutionary publishing office and headquarters for a newly emerging revolutionary counterintelligence bureau; in Geneva, the target was the center of the Socialist Revolutionaries, assigned at first to Maria; and at Brussels, Leo and his wife were to trace how the revolutionaries smuggled arms to Russia. The Beitner team's work was a success under Rataev and under his successors

Paris Okhrana

an outstanding Okhrana achievement against revolutionary smugglers and counterfeiters.[4]

The second team was a married couple named Zagorski. The man reported to headquarters as agent-at-large, traveling almost constantly, while his wife concentrated on the Fighting Unit of the Socialist Revolutionaries in Paris and Germany, reporting through Rataev's office only.[5]

At about the same time the later famous Evno Azev was given to Rataev. He had served in Germany for several years and then been ordered dismissed by Rachkovsky as unreliable, but he was rehired by headquarters when he gained entry to the central committee of the Socialist Revolutionaries and their Fighting Unit of assassins and "expropriators."

The names of some other important penetration agents sent from Russia were Aleksandrov, Chizhikov, Borovskaia, Brodski, Fudim, and Gramm. In addition, Rataev retained all the agents he inherited from Rachkovsky. The only deep-cover agent he himself hired was a Frenchman, August Doré, for a counterespionage assignment in Vienna. This man, however, landed in jail soon after arriving in Austria in 1905 and later caused much trouble by demanding compensation for his six months in prison.

Rataev seldom acted as case officer for the penetration agents. For the most part, they had had years of experience in intelligence operations in Russia, several of them under the personal direction of Zubatov, chief of the Moscow Branch and a master mind in penetration work. Whatever operational guidance they needed in the field was given in headquarters communications. As a rule, however, Rataev would be informed of the identity of the agent and his background, the briefing he had received, the target assigned him, his approximate date of arrival, his pseudonym, and often the recognition passwords to be used.

Overt Staff

Rataev increased his office staff to four men, retaining Chashnikov and Golshman (until the latter's retirement during this period) and adding Ivan Molchanov and Ilin in 1904-1905. They acted as reports officers and also as case officers to the extent of meeting and taking care of new arrivals from Russia.

---

[4] See the "Julietta" case summarized in *Studies* IX 2, p. 26.

[5] See the "Sharzh" case in *Studies* IX 2, p. 38 ff.

~~CONFIDENTIAL~~

Paris Okhrana ~~CONFIDENTIAL~~

The external service during this period acquired only a few new agents but was better systematized by the use of principal agents to lead the networks of non-Russian investigators. Henri Bint, who had served since the days of Korvin-Krukovskoi, became the principal agent in Paris. He maintained constant personal contact with the Sûreté offices and was in charge of surveillance men in France, Switzerland, and the French and Italian Rivieras.[6] Bint's home was also his office for meeting agents and receiving mailed reports. To get his own instructions and pass on information he normally met Chasnikov or Molchanov, never Rataev. Bint's more important detectives of the period were Eugène Invernizzi, first hired in 1899 for investigations in Italy; Albert Sambain and Eugène Leveque in Paris; and Boquet, Rigault, Depassel, and Deleamon in Geneva and other cities of Switzerland.

The most permanent liaison agent in Paris was a man named Fehrenbach whose more than 5,000 identity reports during this period were all copies of Sûreté records on Russian émigrés in France. Their volume indicates that Fehrenbach must have spent most of his working time in the Sûreté offices. The arrangements for this liaison assignment had been made by Rachkovsky, but the bulk of production from it came during Rataev's tenure.

Fringe Operations

The outpost in London, referred to as an agentura in Rataev's dispatches, acquired agents Powells and Michael Thorpe. Powells was a retired Scotland Yard detective recommended to the Okhrana by Thorpe, his former boss and a younger man with similar background. Both had previous experience in operating against Russian revolutionaries in London. The organization of the Berlin agentura remained the same as it had been, with Michael Barkov as case officer for German investigators and Harting handling the Russian penetration agents and high-level liaison with the Prussian Sicherheit Dienst.

Rataev was not at all a political activist like his predecessor. An important political action operation did develop during his term in Paris, but he was at most only a channel for funds, the principal operator receiving all instructions directly from headquarters. This was Ivan F. Manasevich-Manuilov, a nobleman, roving diplomat, and high-level contact man, who as a spotter for the MVD back in the 1890's had had occasional encounters with Rachkovsky. The Okhrana sent

---

[6] Some of his later operations are described in *Studies* IX 3, p. 60 ff.

~~CONFIDENTIAL~~ 65

1. *(Continued)*

him to Paris in 1903 under Ministry of Foreign Affairs cover to resume work started two years previously with an organization called the "Circle of French Journalists." How Manasevich-Manuilov operated with this and another organization, the "League for Saving the Russian Fatherland," is not recorded in Rataev's dispatches. The only references to his activities are the gross amounts of expenditure. These, which reached thousands of rubles monthly, do reveal that newspapers like *Figaro, Echo de Paris,* and *Gaulois* were recipients of subsidies from the operation.

Succession

After mid-1905 the Paris station was to experience a great revival under Arkady Harting. But his is a story that should stand alone.

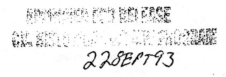

Third chief of the Okhrana's Paris center for combatting the Russian revolutionaries abroad.

THE ILLUSTRIOUS CAREER OF ARKADIY HARTING [1]

Rita T. Kronenbitter

To the Russian revolutionaries of all colors the life of Abraham Hackelman, as he was originally named, was one of endless and utmost infamy. He was a traitor to his ethnic group, an informer, spy, provocateur, impostor, and the most ruthless bloodhound of the Tsarist regime. When his true identity was exposed in 1909 at the height of his career as Arkadiy Harting, the press of western Europe was filled with accounts of his betrayals and activities as a master spy on behalf of the political police and finally as director of its foreign service, the Paris Okhrana. Among the files of the Paris station there are preserved several thick volumes of clippings from European newspapers giving the revolutionaries' version of the life of this extraordinary and by them most hated man. Writers competed with each other in describing him in the strongest terms of dread and repugnance.

The newspapers received the bulk of their information about his sinister exploits from Vladimir Burtzev, who at that time was engaged in setting up a counterintelligence bureau for the revolutionaries. When he first broke the news that Paris Okhrana chief Harting was none other than the former agent provocateur Hackelman,[2] who 19 years before under the alias Landesen had been sentenced in absentia by a Paris tribunal to five years' imprisonment, the press wanted more of such sexy stuff. Burtzev's bureau supplied more. It began issuing special bulletins on the case, for the story constituted a windfall of favorable publicity for the revolutionaries and a damning indictment of the already discredited Paris Okhrana, Burtzev's paramount target. It also brought Burtzev in some needed money; the papers were eager

---

[1] Based chiefly on the collection *Zagranichnaya Okhrana* in the Hoover Institution. For earlier articles from this source see "The Okhrana's Female Agents" Parts I and II, *Studies* IX 2 p. 25 ff and IX 3 p. 59 ff, "Okhrana Agent Dolin," *Studies* X 2 p. 57 ff; and "Paris Okhrana 1885-1905," *Studies* X 3 p. 55 ff.

[2] The Russian, having no "H," transliterates the two names as Garting and Gakelman or Gekelman respectively.

71

to pay for releases about the scandal embarrassing the Russian and indirectly the French government.

While this frenzied publicity was based on two central items of truth—Harting's identity with Hackelman and the 1890 criminal conviction in Paris—the great bulk of it was dizzy flights of fancy, propaganda aimed at the Okhrana when the Tsarist service could not defend itself or enter into polemics with the European press. Hackelman's intelligence career could not have been known to the revolutionaries except in fragmentary incidents, and his story has never been written. The Okhrana files, containing hundreds of his reports and a few about him, however, attest to his truly fantastic rise from a lowly informer to a position dominating the Russian secret service abroad and exerting a strong influence on the services of the European countries. Then after this phenomenal ascent the sudden fall, ending his career forever and hurting seriously the organization he had built.

Petersburg and Riga

Abraham Hackelman was born 29 October 1861 in Pinsk, where his parents owned a small grocery store. It appears that he first served the political police as an informer while in secondary school there. Then, being a very promising student, he was sent to St. Petersburg in 1879 to enroll at the Gorniy Institut. Here he made a good start, devoting himself entirely to his school work. Rather shy and aware that as a Jewish student he had to do exceptionally well to satsify the professors, he avoided student company. Student politics would not only interfere with his studies but also bring a constant risk of expulsion. He was intent on becoming an engineer as soon as possible and was not interested in political agitation, particularly not in the underground cell meetings of the terroristic *Narodnaia Volia* (People's Will) which was concentrating on recruiting students at the time.

Hackelman would most likely have become an engineer if he had not been befriended by two diametrically opposite persons at about the same time. One of these was Vladimir Burtzev, a classmate and student leader, who wanted him to join his underground cell. The other, who did not visit him at school, was Colonel Sekerinsky, chief of the St. Petersburg political police. The details of both the ostensible and the true recruitment are unknown, but it can be assumed that Hackelman would never have joined the subversives except on the colonel's urging. He became a professed fellow conspirator and an informer. His studies apparently did not suffer as much as he had

72

Arkadiy Harting   ███████████

feared, and his small income from the newly constituted Okhrana relieved his struggling parents of the burden of his college expenses.

Gradually Hackelman gained access to the inner circle of conspirators planning terrorist acts. He reported a series of plots and made possible a large number of arrests. Nevertheless he managed to escape suspicion. When he was once mentioned as possibly the traitor, Burtzev, in whose cell he worked, refused to believe it. He held Hackelman to be his best friend and an ideal revolutionary. Defending him in the meetings of the underground, he told the comrades how the two of them had begun together their revolutionary careers. Their careers would in fact run on together, but on opposite sides as principal protagonists in the great battle between the Okhrana and revolutionary intelligence.

Burtzev refused to believe an even more positive accusation against Hackelman. In 1882 the revolutionaries caught up with a Captain Sergei Degaev who had worked among them as an undercover agent for the Okhrana. Degaev declared in his confession that Hackelman was also an Okhrana informer. Luckily no one at the time believed in the truth of this confession.[3] Hackelman continued to be trusted, and more subversives were arrested that year, including finally Burtzev himself when he brought in from Rumania a team equipped with bombs.

To escape any suspicion for this betrayal, Hackelman promptly left St. Petersburg and enrolled in the Riga Polytechnicum. Here he resumed his extracurricular activities, participating in the student underground and reporting to the Okhrana. But when in 1884 a number of arrests were made, the Riga subversives got more on him than a mere suspicion; they uncovered his association with an Okhrana officer and sentenced him to death as a traitor to the cause.

Swiss Interlude

Hackelman escaped abroad and enrolled the same year under the name Landesen at the Polytechnicum in Zurich. He had again decided to devote himself to finishing his college work, but here too he met a group of Russian students, or exiled revolutionaries who made studying something of a sideline. Associating with them, he found

---

[3] Instead of sentencing Degaev to death after his confession, the terrorists ordered him as a matter of retribution to kill his case officer, a Colonel Sudeikin. After accomplishing this murder Degaev escaped abroad and eventually became a teacher of mathematics in the United States.

███████████   73

a whole crew engaged in the manufacture of bombs for delivery to Russia. Two of these amateurs, students of philosophy named Dembsky and Dembo, were blown to pieces by an infernal machine they had just constructed. For nearly a year "Landesen" had no contacts with the Okhrana, whose headquarters at St. Petersburg, however, followed attentively his association with the Narodnaia Volia terrorists in Zurich and Geneva.

The Okhrana had recently decided to establish a center in Paris for operations against the émigré revolutionaries in France and Switzerland. One of its high officials named Zvoliansky was sent abroad late in 1884 for the necessary talks with the French government and also to spot possible recruits for penetration agents. Landesen headed the list of prospects. Zvoliansky, who had known him in St. Petersburg, interviewed him in Zurich and proposed he continue his studies at the university and be given the status of secret agent working in the Narodnaia Volia there. Landesen was willing but asked for a salary of 1,000 francs a month. He also wanted an assignment in Paris, whereas most of the leading Russian terrorists were at that time concentrated in Switzerland. Zvoliansky reported that he had a "talent for the job . . . skillful and intelligent, he could become most useful if he were not asking for such a high salary."

When in April 1885 Peter Rachkovsky was commissioned to head the Paris Okhrana, he was instructed to contact Landesen again for possible recruitment but to negotiate for a salary of not more than 300 francs. He was given a dossier on the candidate's past services with a caveat in regard to his security-mindedness. If recruited, Landesen was to receive an extensive security briefing to preclude any repetition of the 1884 exposure in Riga.

The clandestine meetings with Landesen lasted four days. Rachkovsky, though he had headquarters' and Zvoliansky's assessments to go on and in spite of headquarters' impatience for the immediate recruitment of penetration agents, did not want to rush into hiring people. To size the man up himself, he induced him to talk for two days about his informant jobs at St. Petersburg and Riga and his contacts with the terrorists in Switzerland. His security failures in Russia had to be discussed in detail so that he could recognize his own weaknesses and learn to guard against another exposure. After Landesen's admissions and explanations fully satisfied him, Rachkovsky directed the talks to his prospective employment and assignments. In the end he persuaded him to remain in Switzerland and start at 300 francs a month plus travel expenses. Landesen would report directly

74

Arkadiy Harting

to Rachkovsky, as his case officer, on the activities of the Narodnaia Volia.

Rachkovsky did not rule out the possibility of Landesen's eventual transfer to Paris, but the logical place for the time being was Switzerland, where he had already developed some contact with several rabid subversives. His acquaintances Bach, Baranikova, Sladkova, and Lavrov all had dossiers in Rachkovsky's files of dangerous terrorists. Bach, living in exile since 1880, was one of the most wanted persons; he had been ringleader in several assassinations in Russia. The contents of his dossier were carefully gone over in the course of Landesen's briefing for his first assignment; the agent memorized everything on record about Bach's background, personal character, and past conspiratorial associates.

For a start, Landesen was to rent an apartment in Zurich that would be a convenient meeting place for the subversives. He was to play the role of a student whose family were of some means—not too rich, but putting him in easier circumstances than the average Russian student in Zurich. At first he should associate with all young Russians there, regardless of political attitude, but then gradually show preference for the revolutionaries, particularly Bach and another intellectual named Lev Tikhomirov. Rachkovsky did not reveal to Landesen that the reason for his special interest in Tikhomirov was a plan to develop him into another penetration agent.[4]

Landesen soon became well known in Zurich's colony of Russian students and exiled intellectuals. His associates were often in need, and small loans led them into some dependence on him. The poorest of them all seemed to be Bach, his principal target, and it was not long before Bach agreed to save himself rent by moving into his apartment, which thus became the central meeting place for the terrorist intellectuals in Switzerland. Landesen reported on them and their movements daily. When he asked for more money, Rachkovsky would

---

[4] Lev Tikhomirov was a Nihilist and influential advocate of terror. Landesen's reports on his character and personal weaknesses gave Rachkovsky the background needed for his plan to convert and recruit him. To shake his revolutionary morale Rachkovsky apparently first used poison-pen letters. Then he engaged journalist Jules Hansen to publish a pamphlet in French entitled "Confessions of a Nihilist" which compromised Tikhomirov and made him the target of revolutionary attacks. He was even blamed, thanks to Landesen's machinations, for a police raid on an underground printshop in Geneva which produced tracts for the Narodnaia Volia to smuggle into Russia. In the end he did not become an agent, but Rachkovsky did persuade him to publish a book in Russian, *Why I Stopped Being a Revolutionary.*

comply promptly but always in moderation. The agent could not afford to risk arousing suspicion about his income. His money actually came from Russia, the Okhrana backstopping in the role of his relatives and occasionally writing to reproach him with affection for being a foolish spendthrift.

After an inspection tour in the fall of 1886, Zvoliansky submitted to headquarters a critique of Hackelman-Landesen's first work abroad. He praised both agent and case officer for their teamwork, Rachkovsky in Paris for his guidance and Landesen in Zurich for exhaustive coverage of the terrorists' activities. The Okhrana had received a steady flow of reports on all projects of the leader Bach through his conferences in Landesen's apartment with comrades living in various Swiss cities and those dispatched to or returning from Russia. It had full information on the clandestine Narodnaia Volia printshop in Geneva which produced terrorist literature for smuggling into Russia.

Rachkovsky consulted Landesen about the mounting and timing of a raid on this printshop. Landesen supplied him enough information to convince the Swiss police that they should make such a raid and arrest the subversives. The operation was successful. It terminated the Narodnaia Volia propaganda system, eliminated Switzerland as a center for the terrorist organization, and all but destroyed the organization. Landesen remained in Zurich until 1890 to continue watching Bach and his residual cell.

Provocation in Paris

Landesen's next assignment, as a penetration agent in Paris, was of short duration but in a way the most significant of his career. In this operation he was actually an agent provocateur.[5] His case officer had a very special purpose in mounting the operation; it was a studied auxiliary to a major political action project. None of his records indicate that Rachkovsky formally informed headquarters about his ruthless plan, and it is possible that no one but case officer and agent knew about it. Their teamwork in planning and carrying out this action was even closer than that which Zvoliansky had commended in Switzerland.

---

[5] The term "provokator" was applied by the revolutionaries to all police agents and investigators. In a strict sense, however, this operation appears to be the only one abroad on record which definitely constituted deliberate provocation. The practice was officially forbidden.

76

Arkadiy Harting

By 1890 the majority of the Russian terrorists had moved from Switzerland to Paris. It was natural for Landesen to move there to join his student friends and grateful colleagues. Paris thus became the new underground center. Landesen attended their gatherings and grew to be one of their leaders. His reports told of new plans for acts of terror to be committed in Russia and against Russian officials abroad. In Russia the information would have given ground enough for raiding the meetings or arresting the members individually.

In France, however, Rachkovsky felt helpless. He had gained the close cooperation of the Sûreté, but the French police were handicapped in anti-revolutionary actions by an unfriendly press and public opinion. He therefore planned the next operation with the purpose of helping to sway French public favor away from the revolutionaries and their anti-Tsarist propaganda. More important still, if he could force the Sûreté to act against the terrorists it would impress the regime in St. Petersburg with the French government's ability to crack down on revolutionaries. This last aspect of the operation was probably his main concern. He had put much effort behind the scenes into promoting a Franco-Russian alliance. While the French seemed to favor it, the imperial court in Russia was lukewarm or even hostile so long as France was giving asylum and protection to Nihilists and other enemies of the Tsar.

Case officer and agent played equal roles, as they were accustomed, in planning this politically motivated master stroke. The risk of failure was considered, and the real risk of exposing the provocateur. It was decided that if Landesen were exposed he could go into hiding and then take another identity for his further career. Landesen suggested the plan of operation and Rachkovsky allotted the funds. Landesen was to propose a scheme for the assassination of Tsar Alexander III to a group of leading terrorists. Rachkovsky suggested the names of some that should be assembled for the conspiracy and Landesen added others.

Some twenty-five conspirators assembled for the first meeting and listened to Landesen's scheme. It entailed the construction of bombs in Paris. When the question was raised as to who would pay for the equipment, Landesen said he was sure he could get the necessary sum from his rich uncle. A workshop was rented in the Raincy woods near Paris. Various types of bombs were manufactured and several conspirators trained who were to go to Russia as an advance team. Landesen himself was scheduled to go with this group.

77

When enough bombs were on hand and the first conspirators ready to depart, Landesen set a date when the weapons were to be distributed among the conspirators, together with written instructions on the role each one was to play in the assassinations. Rachkovsky, who was kept informed of every detail, now knew just when and where to find this incriminating evidence in the possession of the individual conspirators, for Landesen was personally in charge of the distribution. Through his agent Jules Hansen, Rachkovsky passed the information to Minister of Foreign Affairs Flourence and Minister of Interior Constance. The Sûreté then rounded up all the participants with their bombs and other arms except Landesen, who had disappeared.

In the ensuing famous Paris trial of 1890, Landesen was sentenced in absentia, as the ringleader, to five years imprisonment; some twenty others were sent to prison or expelled from France. The provocation was a complete success from Rachkovsky's standpoint except for the effect on his most important agent. The court trial was useful in alerting the French public to the dangers of the Russian terrorists. The incident promoted liaison with the Sûreté Générale, which got credit for rounding up the subversives and so enhanced its reputation for good work. The Paris center was commended by headquarters. Above all, the imperial regime was now convinced that the French government could be depended upon to be firm and take action against the Nihilists. Negotiations for signing a Franco-Russian alliance began shortly after the trial.

International Honors

Landesen remained in his Paris hideout for two months after the arrests. In August 1890, settling in Belgium as a Russian nobleman, he received an award of 1,000 rubles' annual pension. This did not mean retirement. At one time he was reported active with a Baron Sternberg, an Okhrana agent sent from headquarters to work among the Belgian Anarchists. For the most part, however, he traveled on Okhrana business through various European countries, usually as a security companion to important personages. In a letter from London still preserved in the files he asked headquarters' permission to get himself baptized in the Russian Orthodox Church and to have his name legally changed to Baron Arkadiy Mikhailovich Harting. The request was granted; he became an Orthodox Christian at Wiesbaden, but the festival ceremony took place at the Embassy Church in Berlin, with Count Muraviev officiating as his godfather and the wife of Imperial Senator Mansurov as godmother. For this purpose he falsely

78

Arkadiy Harting

registered his birthplace as St. Petersburg. He did not feel comfortable in this company as a Jew from Pinsk.

In recognition for his extraordinary services Rachkovsky heaped favor after favor upon Harting, usually in the form of important assignments that could only lead to promotions and decorations of all sorts. When Crown Prince Aleksandrovich came for his betrothal to Allissa Hesse in Coburg-Gotha, Harting, in charge of security, received a present of 1,000 rubles, together with an appropriate medal. As the Tsar's bodyguard in Copenhagen he was given medals from the Emperor and from the King of Denmark; and when the Tsar went hunting in Sweden and Norway he got gold medals there. Similar assignments in Germany, Austria-Hungary, and other countries invariably brought presents, medals, or other decorations. He earned several medals in England and France. Now one of the most decorated of contemporary international dignitaries, he traded his dashing socialite bachelorhood for marriage to a young and very wealthy Belgian, Madeleine Palot.

It appears that the decorations and prestige and even the marriage to a rich socialite were all part of a design. Rachkovsky was after firm liaison arrangements with the security services of as many European countries as possible. When he had put an ace operator of the Okhrana into the position of being awarded presents and decorations from all these governments, he could reciprocate and honor their security officials with awards from the Tsar. Medals exchanged in an atmosphere of friendship and mutual recognition often paved the way to cooperation. It was in fact in this period of the 1890's, as a sequel to Harting's international assignments, that Rachkovsky succeeded in establishing liaison between the various security services and his Okhrana center. And it was in Belgium, after Harting's marriage, that the Okhrana developed the most lasting and comprehensive exchange of information. Up to the outbreak of war in 1914 the Paris center received from the Belgian Sûreté Générale a continuous transcript of its records on all Russian political subversives and other terrorists.

Rachkovsky had been trying for some time to establish a separate agentura in Berlin. The city was becoming a center for the Russian Social Democrats in exile, who used the Prussian borders with Russia's Poland as a safe and convenient infiltration gate for revolutionaries. The Prussian Sicherheit Dienst was hesitant about developing permanent liaison with the Okhrana, and it refused to discuss a separate agentura, even if the agents were to be Germans, until Rachkovsky

79

specified that the proposed station would be under the direction of Harting and its task limited to collecting information on Russian revolutionaries and supplying this to the Germans for purposes of cooperation. The Praesidium approved the proposal without delay upon hearing the name Harting, a man who had been decorated by their Kaiser and thanks to whom several of the Praesidium officials were wearing the Tsar's medals.

Station Berlin

Harting assumed the Berlin post in December 1900. Settling down at Friedrichstrasse No. 4, he was known as an engineer attached to the Imperial Consulate. He opened the agentura on the same pattern as the center in Paris, engaging first three and soon thereafter three more external, surveillance agents and then gradually introducing the internal, penetration agents. On the average he had to maintain three safe houses, since he and his assistant Michael Barkov had to make all their intelligence contacts outside the consulate.

The external agents were men recommended by or at least known to the German security police. Despite this advantage they never gained the access their counterparts in other countries had to police records on the revolutionaries. The reason for this, Harting explained in several dispatches, was the German system of decentralization. There was not only a separate and independent service in each state of the Reich, but within Prussia and even in Berlin each police district kept its separate file and there was no routine reporting to a central intelligence repository. To overcome this difficulty Harting hired as his secret agent Herr Wineck, a high official of the Sicherheit Dienst and former chief of its Russian section. Wineck was in a position to gather the police records on the revolutionaries from all districts, and between 1902 and 1904 he channeled over a thousand reports to Harting. He was paid for this service in the form of gifts; a regular salary did not seem appropriate.[*]

Harting maintained in Germany some half dozen penetration agents, frequently assigning them to border infiltration points. His ace man was Dr. Yakob Zhitomirsky, who as a student in Berlin had worked for the Sicherheit Dienst before he was picked up by the agentura.

---

[*] In the version given by V. A. Agafonov, Wineck, wrongly called Winen, is shown serving Harting with the express approval of Kaiser Wilhelm. Harting's dispatches requesting headquarters not to award a medal to Wineck because such favors might compromise him clearly disprove this story.

80

Arkadiy Harting ██████████████████

in 1902 and insinuated into the Leninist group of revolutionaries. His exceptional achievements were culminated in 1906, after Harting had become chief of the Paris center.

Rachkovsky's concept of the Berlin agentura was as a branch of the Paris center with operations limited to Germany and the Low Countries. As long as the chief in Paris was Harting's protector and real friend the arrangement worked smoothly, but Rachkovsky fell into disfavor and was replaced by a bureaucrat named Rataev who, in Harting's estimate, lacked all the qualifications of an intelligence director.[7] Harting's agents therefore were soon found on special assignments in Switzerland, Italy, and England. The resulting friction with Paris never came to a head, although a sudden summons to St. Petersburg once made Harting wonder whether he was going to get a reprimand for projecting operations into Rataev's territory.

Japanese Targets

The call to headquarters turned out to be the beginning of a new chapter in Harting's career. Director Lopukhin had read with interest a number of Harting's agents' reports concerning the activities of a Japanese Colonel Akashi, who was conducting anti-Russian intelligence operations from Paris into several European capitals. The director wanted Harting to help set up a separate counterespionage organization aimed at Akashi's system. His job as chief in Berlin was abruptly terminated and a caretaker sent there.

Harting now became a traveling staff agent. In constant trips back and forth from St. Petersburg he repeatedly covered Paris, Stockholm, Copenhagen, Brussels, and London. His task was to spot among the diplomatic missions agents that could develop access to the Japanese embassies and consulates. He concentrated especially on the Japanese legation at Brussels, where he learned that Colonel Akashi was spending more time than at his regular post in Paris. It may have been Harting's trusted Belgian friends who got hold of the Japanese code for telegraphic messages.[8]

Returning from these many trips abroad he made until late 1904, Harting was debriefed not only by the Okhrana director but also by

---

[7] For Rataev's administration see *Studies* X 3 p. 62 ff.

[8] The operation which exploited the code and developed a network for intercepting messages in a telegraph office in Brussels was entrusted to Okhrana official Ivan Manasevich-Manuilov, who used 16 agents in the daring and for a time most successful operation. For an earlier operation of Manasevich-Manuilov see *Studies* X 3, p. 65 f.

██████████████   81

the general staff. Russia was at war with Japan, and the military intelligence section developing new assets gave Harting a field officer status. His rank was raised nearly every time he came back from Europe. In the end he was given the stars of a major general, assigned to the regular army, and placed in charge of a newly formed counterespionage unit for the Far East. The Okhrana files, logically, contain no record of his work on this military assignment, which was of short duration before the sudden termination of hostilities.

Revival in Paris

In August 1905 the MVD appointed Harting chief of the foreign Okhrana. His friend Rachkovsky, now back in favor, was made chief of operations at headquarters. The same teamwork the two had displayed in the past reappeared at once, now at the top level. Rachkovsky gave Harting authority to organize the service according to his best judgment. As the correspondence shows, Harting's instructions were to study the structure of the service and the productivity of operations, report his findings, suggest changes, and proceed with whatever measures he deemed necessary.

Harting proved to be a truly methodical organizer. On the way to Paris he stopped in Berlin to close the agentura there—it had practically stopped functioning in his absence—and transfer its records to Paris. The key agents in Germany, however, he left under the direction of case officer Barkov.

In Paris, Harting found that Rataev had already left for Russia in order to avoid meeting his hostile successor. The Paris establishment had all but disintegrated. The one remaining deep-cover agent, Gersh Kuryansky, was reporting direct to the Okhrana office, contrary to strict rules against such practices. Only four external agents were left, of which only two could be used for surveillance purposes; one, Fehrenbach, did nothing but collect information from liaison centers, and another, Henri Bint, had become a confidential aide and principal agent and refused to go back to routine surveillance assignments.[9]

Harting made visits to Geneva and London. In Geneva Swiss security chief Mercier was placing intercepted correspondence of the revolutionaries at the disposal of Okhrana agents Rigault and Depassel. But two other agents, police employees Boquet and Deleamon, did nothing but deliver transcripts of police records. There were no sur-

---

[9] For these arrangements under Rataev see *Studies* X 3, p. 65.

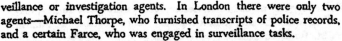

Arkadiy Harting

veillance or investigation agents. In London there were only two agents—Michael Thorpe, who furnished transcripts of police records, and a certain Farce, who was engaged in surveillance tasks.

In Harting's first survey he reported to headquarters that not only the external service but also the Russian clerks in the Okhrana office were being paid through the Frenchman Bint, who in fact even kept the office accounts. Bint was paying himself up to 1,000 francs a month, and the pay of all external agents had been greatly increased—without justification, because at least during the last twelve months they had been almost inactive. The payment of these exorbitant salaries left no money to pay a newly arrived deep-cover agent, Batushansky. Harting demanded a free hand to revise the budget, establish a substantial penetration service, and run an invigorated external service. Headquarters approved, and he brought under his control the penetration agents who had been sent out by the provincial Okhrana branches and at the same time began recruiting in the field.[10]

Within a year Harting had succeeded in placing 16 productive penetration agents in the Anarchist, Socialist Revolutionary, and Social Democratic committees in France, Switzerland, Germany, and England. He developed strong liaison ties with the security services of many countries, and wherever possible he used external agents who were approved by the local services and therefore given access to their security records on Russian revolutionaries.

Arms Smuggling

One of Harting's major achievements was to completely stop gun-running into Russia on the part of the revolutionaries. For this purpose he set up a network of special agents to find and report on anyone financing or purchasing arms, the dealers involved, the vessels carrying the cargoes, their captains and crews, etc. Seven such agents were assigned to the ports Amsterdam-Rotterdam, Antwerp, London-Birmingham, Hall, Liverpool, and Geneva. He also had paid informants in the companies engaged in arms shipping, and he developed contacts with chiefs of the secret police in Hamburg, Lübeck, and other ports.

---

[10] In an outgoing dispatch he took note, however, that agent Vinogradov (Evno Azev) had not been transferred to his control but was being paid directly from headquarters.

83

Arkadiy Harting

The smuggling problem had become acute during the Russo-Japanese War, when Colonel Akashi supplied Konni Zilliacus, the Finnish Socialist, funds to purchase guns for a shipment on the SS "John Crafton." It is not certain that Harting had a man aboard this ship, but at any rate he was able to inform headquarters of its cargo and schedule in time to prevent its docking and unloading, and the cargo was lost when the steamer later grounded in the delta of the Kem River. Thereafter his agents uncovered other attempted shipments— on the "Luma," "Flynn," "Cecile," and "Cysne," one steamer after another. All the attempts failed.

As all shipments through the Baltic were blocked, the Leninist group in Berlin under the management of Meyer Wallach (Maxim Litvinov) attempted a shipment of arms via the Black Sea. The Dutch security director was the first to inform Harting of the revolutionaries' intent to use this alternate route, sending arms overland via Passau through Austria to the coast. Agent Dr. Zhitomirsky in Berlin was alerted. He soon reported that Litvinov was traveling with eight "seamen" from Berlin to Vienna. Harting put a surveillance agent on the train, and another joined him in Vienna. They reported that Litvinov's group had split into three teams and the first was bound for Bulgaria. Harting rightly guessed that their steamer would be located at the Burgas or Varna docks. He so reported, and the craft was sunk in the Black Sea soon after leaving port.

Organization

The development of the Paris Okhrana into a service which was in operational aspects an independent establishment paralleling the organization in Russia can be attributed predominantly to Harting. Under his direction all previously autonomous assets aboard—in Berlin, the Balkans, and Galicia—were integrated with the Paris center. Within a short period of time the service reached its height of operational activity, and Harting still had only four assistants—his number-two man Boris Sushkov, Ivan Molchanov and Nikolai Chashnikov taken over from Rataev, and Ivan Melnikov. Sushkov and Molchanov often served as case officers for internal agents; Melnikov and Chashnikov worked on records and reports and as contacts with the principals of the external service.

Although Harting, himself a tireless case officer, was thus assisted by two qualified subordinates in maintaining operational contacts with agents, by 1907 the work load and security considerations called for some reorganization. A new type of case officer was introduced, a

84

Arkadiy Harting ███████████

staff officer of gendarme (or army) rank assigned to the field under deep cover to take charge of penetration operatives. Like the deep-cover agents, these new case officers were never admitted to Okhrana premises, and all their contacts with Harting and his aides were clandestine. Captains Dolgov and Andreev were the first such officers, each handling a group of penetration agents. The job required much travel, since the agents might be in England, Switzerland, Italy, or wherever. Dolgov's assignments were usually in England and the Low Countries and Andreev's in France, Switzerland, and Italy, while Michael Barkov continued in Germany.

By the end of 1908 the Paris center had over forty men and women placed in Russian revolutionary organizations abroad, a number of them on some central committee and among the leaders, others at intermediate levels of a conspiratorial hierarchy. Mere membership in a revolutionary party did not qualify for agent work; at least good prospects of gaining influence were required, and of course the confidence of the leaders. The external, detective service was numerically about one-half the size of the internal.

Henri Bint served as the principal for most external agents in France and Switzerland. He also organized teams for special surveillance and investigative jobs and assembled, dispatched, and paid the agents. The constant reshuffling of teams in time made all Bint's agents acquainted with one another. Ordinarily a team under Eugene Invernizzi concentrated on revolutionaries who lived in the Italian and French Rivieras, surveilling them and intercepting their mail through access to local post offices; and similar teams were at work in Berlin and London. All of them, however, were subject to disruption when some member of the imperial family needed protection on a visit in western Europe. Quite often Bint was ordered to call together some dozen agents and organize them for coordinated operations with the police and security units of the area to be visited. On such assignments Bint or whoever was in charge in his stead would be in constant telegraphic communication with Harting, informing him hour by hour of the placement of each agent, coordination arrangements, alerts, warnings, etc.

One of Harting's major contributions to the organization of the Paris office was the introduction of a filing system and a system for recording intelligence and operational data. During his period of office, headquarters began to supply printed 3x5 cards on all revolutionaries and political suspects. Harting supplemented these with additional data and started an operational card file on all persons

███████

85

mentioned in intelligence and operational reports. This reference system, as numerous notations indicate, was used for operational planning, verification of data, and background for intelligence reporting. The Paris files thus became in some respects superior to those in the central Okhrana repository in Russia.

The Fall

Of the four chiefs of the Paris Okhrana Harting seems the most impressive in both activity and personality, and he was no doubt the most universally liked by his office subordinates and secret agents. The same kind of teamwork he had achieved with Rachkovsky he extended to his agents. What endeared him to them more than the remuneration—which he always insisted on keeping at high levels wherever due—was his engaging personality and habitual human interest in their welfare and security.

The abrupt end of Harting's service came as a very serious blow to the Okhrana abroad. He himself probably expected it after Leonid Menshchikov, a former subordinate official of the Okhrana in Russia, defected to Vladimir Burtzev and the intelligence bureau he was organizing for the revolutionaries. Harting suspected rightly that Menshchikov had some information which might lead to his exposure. On the morning of 15 June 1909 the Paris newspapers broke the sensational news that Arkadiy Mikhailovich Harting, chief of the Russian secret police in Paris, famous socialite, and candidate for the French Legion of Honor, was none other than that Abraham Hackelman who, under the alias Landesen, had been sentenced in 1890 by a Paris tribunal to five years imprisonment as a terrorist provocateur. The press demanded his immediate arrest and Socialist deputy Jaurès seized on the case in parliament to attack the Clemenceau cabinet and call for the expulsion of the Russian secret service.

The government in St. Petersburg issued official denials, pointing to Harting's noble birth, high rank in the army, etc. but at the same time sent telegrams ordering him to leave Paris at once. He settled at first in Belgium under some unknown name. Burtzev sent teams to Brussels to locate and kidnap him to bring him back to France and prison. But Harting hid so well this time that he even vanished from the secret Okhrana files.

86

3. The Sherlock Holmes of the Revolution

How a self-appointed counterintelligence expert fought the Tsar's political police on behalf of the Russian revolutionaries abroad.

THE SHERLOCK HOLMES OF THE REVOLUTION

Rita T. Kronenbitter[1]

Vladimir Lvovich Burtzev, active chiefly as a revolutionary propagandist in Petersburg and abroad after the failure of the 1905 uprising, had been a leading terrorist twenty and more years earlier. Now, though venerated by the younger generation of insurgents for his past achievements and appreciated for his present propaganda services, he was considered too meek and gentle to mix into current terrorist plotting. He was never a member of any of the numerous revolutionary committees nor admitted to the inner councils. He was above all not privy to the dead secrecy of assassination conspiracies.

He developed a genius for counterintelligence investigation, however, that was to overcome this isolation and raise him again to a central position among the revolutionaries. He had the perspective of decades of subversive work. He pondered the failures of revolutionary conspiracies in the early 1880's, the betrayals of his own and other carefully planned operations, and the treacheries inspired by the police among prisoners and Siberian exiles. He had learned much of Okhrana practices the hard way, from the numerous interrogations to which he and his comrades were subjected in Russia. Later, permanently settled in Paris, he was to start keeping notes, organizing in folders information on past and current episodes and maintaining his own dossiers on fellow revolutionaries as well as Okhrana and police officials. He needed such files in his work as journalist and propa-

---

[1] Based, except for the story of Evno Azef's exposure, for which secondary sources like Agafonov and Nikolaevsky were used, principally on the files of the Okhrana's Paris station which are preserved in the Hoover Institution at Stanford. For earlier *Studies* articles from this source see the author's "The Okhrana's Female Agents," IX 2 p. 25 ff and IX 3 p. 59 ff, "Okhrana Agent Dolin," X 2 p. 57 ff, "Paris Okhrana 1885-1905," X 3 p. 55 ff, and "The Illustrious Career of Arkadiy Harting," XI 1 p. 71 ff.

83

ganda writer, but they would also provide a basis for his first intelligence investigations.

Whiffs of Treachery

In 1905 an unknown, veiled woman delivered a letter to a member of the underground at Petersburg which claimed that the Okhrana had two spies in the Socialist Revolutionaries' Combat Unit, a certain T., ex-convict, and the engineer Azev, a Jew recently arrived from abroad. Since Evno Azev was actually the top leader of the Combat Unit and the party's chief organizer of terror, the letter was dismissed by the revolutionaries as obviously an Okhrana trick. Azev himself, however, recognized the ex-convict T. as Tatarov, whom he knew to be another Okhrana penetration. He was anxious to deflect the threat to his own position and so urged an inquiry. Tatarov, interrogated by a commission, admitted nothing that would lead to proof of his betrayal, but he contradicted himself enough to increase the suspicion against him. He was suspended from the party and finally, on Azev's motion, shot in his home at Kiev.

Burtzev studied the Tatarov case. He realized that it would be preposterous for the Central Committee to prefer charges against Azev; on the other hand, Azev's furious insistence that Tatarov be killed struck him as excessive. There were ample indications in new denunciations and in the failure of planned terroristic acts that there was still, with Tatarov dead, a traitor in the party. Studying the failures, Burtzev noted that almost as a rule at assassination attempts, whether successful or not, Azev was never on the scene. He was the only person witting and involved in the projects of all teams; yet when arrests sooner or later hit each of them, he always succeeded in evading the police.

To give voice to any doubt about Azev, however, would be equivalent to sacrilege, an insult to the party and its romantic terrorists. To the great majority of the members he was its great hero. Burtzev knew that any statement of his suspicions would be considered slanderous, perhaps a deliberate calumny sponsored by the Okhrana.

In 1908 an agent of the Warsaw Okhrana who had decided to defect, Mikhail Bakai, approached Burtzev in Petersburg in his position as editor of the revolutionary journal *Byloe* (The Past). He offered a mass of information about the Okhrana and its Warsaw office that convinced Burtzev of his bona fides. Burtzev talked him into staying in place a little longer, until he had collected more information

84

Sherlock Holmes

on the identities of secret agents. This gamble almost failed; soon thereafter Bakai was arrested and sent to Siberia. But he escaped and came again to Burtzev. Among the new information he had acquired was the identity of the penetration agent who had reported his intention to defect and so caused his arrest. His name was Raskin.

The revolutionaries did not know that Raskin was the Okhrana's name for Azev; still, this was a pointer for Burtzev. Only a few of the top revolutionary leaders had been told of Bakai's defection in place, and of these only Azev had been in Warsaw at the time. Then one day in Petersburg, at a time when the police were arresting revolutionaries right and left, Burtzev saw Azev riding in an open cab. How could Azev, leader of the Combat Unit, ride around the capital in broad daylight? The hypothesis that Raskin and Azev were one and the same person was inescapable.

Hot Pursuit

Soon thereafter Burtzev moved to Paris and started a full-time investigation. He collected further evidence pointing to a traitor at the top of the party, and he was determined to prove that the traitor was Azev. He worked partly by the process of elimination, clearing one leader after another of suspicion until only Azev remained. Even though he was still without concrete proofs he began to voice suspicion openly. But no party leader believed him; Azev continued to direct the party's terrorist activities.

When a party conference opened in London in August 1908, Burtzev wrote to a friend attending it a letter in which he accused Azev of treachery. The letter came to the knowledge of the Central Committee, which decided to take action—against Burtzev. Regardless of how well meant they were, these libels had to stop. Some wanted to arraign him for trial before the underground tribunal; others thought that a frank talk with him might be sufficient. Boris Savinkov, Azev's assistant, was chosen to talk to the misguided old fellow. Boris met with Vladimir Lvovich and told him in confidence what Azev's real role had been in various Combat Unit projects, revealing operational information that was entirely new to Burtzev. This briefing actually only added further circumstantial evidence that strengthened the case against Azev.

Realizing that he would have to have something more than circumstantial evidence, Burtzev executed a masterful operation. He learned that A. A. Lopukhin, dismissed director of the Okhrana, was in Ger-

85

3. *(Continued)*

Sherlock Holmes

many. He had met him in Petersburg on several occasions and guessed that he was now probably disgruntled with the Okhrana and might be willing to talk. He contrived to run into Lopukhin, completely "by accident," on a train from Berlin to Cologne. The old revolutionary showed his embarrassment at the impropriety of imposing his company on a former director of the Okhrana. His gentle excuses and congenial indecision broke the ice, and Lopukhin invited him to share his compartment. Their long conversation eventually turned to the subject of provocateurs used, in spite of the official ban on them, by the Okhrana. Burtzev brought up Raskin as an example, but Lopukhin said he had never heard of him. Only just before they reached Cologne, with more prompting and after some hesitation, he revealed that the only provocateur he ever knew about was a certain engineer named Azev.

Burtzev rushed back to Paris and prepared an open letter, set in type, for members of the Party of Socialist Revolutionaries. He sent a galley proof to the Central Committee. Without naming Lopukhin as the source—he had promised not to—he claimed proof positive that Okhrana agent Raskin and the chief of the Combat Unit were one and the same person.

Disgrace and Triumph

Now the Central Committee had to take formal measures. It appointed three of the most popular revolutionaries as judges—Prince Kropotkin, Vera Figner, and G. A. Lopatin—to try not Azev but Burtzev, for his unwarranted accusations. All the leaders participated, most of them attacking the accuser energetically and more convincingly than he could reply. His evidence appeared only circumstantial, based mostly on police rumors. Vera Figner went so far as to suggest that he should commit suicide. In this predicament he felt obliged to break his promise to Lopukhin; he told in detail about their meeting on the train.

Burtzev was exonerated, but some of the leaders were still skeptical: Lopukhin's statement could have been a police tactic to embarrass and confuse the revolutionaries. Prince Kropotkin decided that a further investigation should be undertaken, and Central Committee member Andrei Argunov was sent to Petersburg to verify Lopukhin's statement. Meanwhile Azev himself learned what had happened and hurried to Petersburg to get General A. V. Gerasimov, his case officer, to have the charge repudiated. So when Argunov visited Lopukhin,

86

50

Sherlock Holmes   ████████████

the latter not only confirmed what he had told Burtzev but also revealed that both Azev and General Gerasimov had put pressure on him to retract.

Burtzev's long fight against handicaps ended on 5 January 1909, when the majority of the Central Committee voted an immediate death sentence. A minority, however, which still hoped that Azev might somehow clear himself, won a postponement of the execution and thus gave him a chance to escape.

The Azev case was only the beginning of a flood of exposures. Bakai had brought the names or aliases of thirty-odd agents connected with the Okhrana's Warsaw branch. Moreover, an Okhrana headquarters staff officer, Leonid Menshchikov, had also defected just before Bakai. Although he had only the code names and fragmentary information on the activities of penetration agents, he provided leads that Burtzev patiently pursued until in June of 1909 he could announce to the world that the celebrated socialite Arkadiy Harting, who as head of the Okhrana abroad was chiefly responsible for its prestige in Western Europe, was actually a miserable little provocateur and since 1890 a fugitive from French justice for his part in a terrorist plot. Paris Okhrana never recovered fully from this blow.

Thus Burtzev, once looked upon as an obnoxious meddler, a disgruntled has-been making irresponsible accusations, became the heroic "Sherlock Holmes of the Russian Revolution" and chief adversary of the Okhrana as counterintelligence officer first for the Social Revolutionaries and their Combat Unit, then for the Leninist Social Democrats, the Anarcho-Communists, and other groups. His triumphant operations would before long begin to turn sour, but in the meantime they had their day.

The Opposition Enlisted

After his permanent move to Paris in 1908, Burtzev maintained a residence at 116 rue de la Glacière until October 1914. From the beginning this apartment served also as his editorial office, first for the weekly *Byloe*, then for *Budushchee* (The Future). It was thus here that he met party leaders, members of various committees, and the general public and kept his library and intelligence files. As his intelligence activities expanded, however, he rented several other offices and also made operational use of the quarters of his principal assistants, initially Mikhail Bakai and the lawyer and journalist Valerian Agafonov.

████████████   87

3. *(Continued)*

Burtzev's triumph had been due partly to Agafonov and a split among Socialist Revolutionaries. The party's Central Committee had been formed in Paris under the leadership of a few exiled revolutionaries of considerable wealth such as Viktor Chernov and Mark Natanson. In frequent conflict with these leaders were a number of professional people, lawyers and journalists in exile, most of them struggling for their livelihood. These, like Burtzev, considered the leaders too lax and complacent about the possibility of Okhrana penetrations. In 1908 they were organized as an "Opposition Group" of about a hundred members by Agafonov, who started publishing their small journal, *Revolutsionnaia Mysl* (Revolutionary Thought). Agafonov was assisted by Gnatovsky and Yudelevsky.

Burtzev joined the Group at once and published in the new journal an article, entitled "Black Book of the Russian Liberation Movement," concerning exposed Okhrana agent Mechislav Kensitski and others accused of being traitors to the revolution; this was the beginning of his campaign against penetrations. More importantly, he thus acquired the leaders of the opposition as his voluntary assistants and agents, who gathered frequently in secret meetings and brought him information on the doings and contacts of all the active revolutionaries.

Okhrana chief Harting was, until his own exposure, fully informed of these developments and the progress of Burtzev's debriefing of defectors Menshchikov and Bakai. He had a penetration who was a member of the Opposition Group and so in constant touch with Burtzev and Agafonov. This agent now reported further that the Group, instead of searching in toto for spies and traitors, was forming a smaller special unit named the "Group of the Activist Minority" to watch closely the party members suspected of treason. Agafonov and Ankel Yudelevsky headed this select body and reported to Burtzev daily.

Secret Police Organized

Bakai, a shrewd and fanatical man who had very personal rather than ideological reasons for wanting to clobber the Okhrana, was selected for a key job in Burtzev's service. Lodging was found for him in a semi-deserted house whose remaining occupants, including the concierge, were all Socialists. The location at 7 rue du Montsouris, a dead-end street, was such that any surveillance of the premises by the Okhrana or the French *Sûreté* would be immediately noticed by the occupants. Paris Okhrana could therefore not comply with

88

52

headquarters' insistence that it watch the place, according to a dispatch it sent to Petersburg. Here Bakai, with the help of Nikolai Sofronski, established what was first reported as his *Liga Politsii* (Police League) but later referred to as the "Revolutionary Police Department."

Bakai's Liga was a covert arm for Burtzev, who apparently did not trust his own office to be free of Okhrana agents (as it actually never was). The Liga was so completely conspiratorial that even important members of the party were not given its address. Its task was to collect intelligence on the Okhrana and its agents and to investigate clandestinely the life of every member of the Party of Socialist Revolutionaries, his income, associations, and loyalty to the cause. Harting expressed to headquarters his prescient apprehension about the Liga's activities and urged that all measures be taken to expel Bakai and Burtzev, as well as Agafonov and other "Activist Minority" leaders, from France. He argued that neither in England nor in Switzerland could such revolutionary counterintelligence efforts cause as much damage as in France.

In Okhrana terminology the task of Agafonov's Activist Minority was essentially internal, penetration of the Okhrana's penetrations, while Bakai's Liga was largely external, doing surveillance and detective-type investigations. Both units reported directly to Burtzev. Both of them, along with Burtzev's own office on the rue de la Glacière, at first depended for support on the not large and not affluent Opposition Group. The funds were meager, but the agents were for the most part avid volunteers, often with moderate incomes of their own.

Vladimir Lvovich Burtzev, from an Okhrana "Man Wanted" bulletin.

3. *(Continued)*

Prosperity: French Agents

The exposure of Evno Azev first impressed on the party leaders the need for a strong counterintelligence establishment to clear their ranks of traitors, and the Harting scandal that followed close on its heels put them solidly behind Vladimir Lvovich. His counterintelligence research had driven their most feared and hated enemy from Paris, leaving the Okhrana office there demoralized and without a chief. His propaganda campaign in Harting's wake filled much of the European press and swayed public opinion. He was behind the parliamentary interpellations that threatened the imperial service with expulsion from France and other countries.

Money flowed in freely for a time, first from the Party of Socialist Revolutionaries, then from other revolutionary groups in Europe and in North America. These funds made it possible for Burtzev to expand the service in several ways. He himself could make operational tours in Europe and one to the United States. He was able to pay the agents in Bakai's Liga and to cover their travel expenses, even on detective assignments to Belgium, England, and Italy. He set up another, separate external service. He had recognized what the Paris Okhrana office had discovered a generation before, that Russians were poorly qualified to tail fellow Russians in France. Regardless of how well they spoke French, they were too readily recognized to be used for surveillance. French agents were available, but they had to be paid regular salaries. Now he could begin to hire some.

The first Frenchman Burtzev hired was Maurice Leroy. Already a detective with years of experience, Leroy had been hired by the Paris Okhrana as one of its principal external agents and entrusted over a half dozen years with many intelligence assignments in France, Germany, and Switzerland. He had worked as a leader of surveillance teams and so knew personally most of the Okhrana's external agents in those countries. He had been dismissed in 1908 because of friction with other principal agents and also on account of his dissipated life and misuse of the Okhrana's money. He was probably Burtzev's only French agent with some motivation beside mere salary, for he wanted to avenge himself, first against Henri Bint and Bittard-Monin, the Okhrana's principal external agents, then against the imperial service in general for firing him.

For Burtzev's emerging intelligence service Leroy was a veritable windfall. He was a mature operator, and he knew all the tricks and methods of the Okhrana's external teams and their liaison contacts.

90

Sherlock Holmes

He knew by name and even address the agents in France and in other countries. From his accounts of his past work Burtzev was able to deduce the pattern of Okhrana surveillance targets. Although he could produce no information on the identities of penetration agents, his voluminous reports on his external tasks provided certain leads even in that direction.

Expanded Services

After several weeks of debriefing, Burtzev designated Leroy in April 1909 the leader of a team of four surveillance agents—a Frenchman named Gandon whom Leroy himself recommended and three young Russians fluent in French, Klepikov, Dolinin, and Komorsky. The job of this team, at the time referred to as "Leroy's Brigade," was almost entirely surveillance and detective investigation (*filature*). Burtzev saw to it that Leroy's work was coordinated with that of Bakai's Liga. The latter undertook the more aggressive investigations, such as searching the premises of suspected Russians, intercepting mail by bribing landlords, checking on contacts among high-level revolutionaries, arresting and interrogating suspects. (One female agent named Ovsianikova in the Liga had a task of internal nature, circulating among the leaders of the party and reporting on their talks and contacts. She joined Burtzev and Bakai on a trip to the Italian Riviera to visit certain well-to-do Socialist Revolutionaries and made observations on their loyalty and support of the revolutionary cause.) Leroy's people, on the other hand, engaged mostly in street surveillance, following suspects, watching their domiciles, and the like.

In a number of operations during 1909 Burtzev arranged for the two external units, or at least their leaders, to work together. When it was learned that Harting was living incognito somewhere in Belgium, Burtzev quickly worked out a plan to locate him and if possible bring him clandestinely back to France, where the police would be alerted to arrest him. Burtzev thought this course would be of greatest propaganda value for the revolutionaries, but if kidnaping and delivery to France were impossible, they could carry out in Belgium the death sentence of their underground tribunal. Bakai and Leroy spent some three months of late 1909 in Belgium with their agents, Bakai investigating at Verviers, Leroy at Liège. They were confident of eventual success, but Harting had been informed of their assignment even before they left Paris.

91

Burtzev's service underwent continuous growth up to 1911. Leroy, in charge of recruiting and handling French agents, became his first deputy. In spite of continuous penetration by the Okhrana he did effective work, in 1913 forcing the adversary to dissolve its external service completely. He hired a number of its dismissed French agents, but most of these were doubled back by the Okhrana. Bakai's Liga was eliminated in 1911; Bakai quarreled with Burtzev over credit for the exposures they both contributed to. Agafonov's "Group of the Activist Minority" somehow lost its identity and is not mentioned after 1910, but Agafonov himself continued active and the number of internal agents working among the revolutionary groups increased.

Some Operations: Kuryansky

Burtzev was a most aggressive operator. He did not wait for leads to put him on the track of traitors; he created situations to produce the leads. Early in April of 1912, for example, Paris Okhrana received two letters, one addressed to the ambassador and the other to the consul general, from unknown persons offering their services as agents. Not suspecting that both were written by Burtzev's service, the Okhrana wrote back giving the two applicants appointments at different times and places. It even gave one a second appointment in response to a plea that the first reply had arrived too late. Neither of the two ever showed up.

But two of the addresses proposed for the meetings were, as Burtzev had suspected, used also for the mailed reports of penetration agents. His only purpose in the fake applications had been to obtain such addresses. His surveillance men now went to work and intercepted the mail for them, which gave him the code names of two Okhrana agents, Karpo and Kodak.

Leroy was able to determine that Kodak, who had a Paris address, was Leiba Poznansky, just recently recruited by the Okhrana. But Karpo's letters showed a London return address. Burtzev's men borrowed several of them and copied the contents before returning them to the post office for delivery. (The Okhrana noted the delay in their receipt but failed to take warning.)

When Burtzev thought he had learned enough about Karpo from his correspondence, he sent a telegram to the London address, inviting him to come to the railroad station to meet a certain train. The agent, true name Gersh Kuryansky, came to this meeting. Burtzev

92

approached him and explained that Petersburg had designated him his new case officer. He asked Kuryansky about his operation and any recently obtained information, and he set the following day for another meeting at his lodging. Kuryansky, suspicious of this new case officer, immediately moved to different quarters. Burtzev, finding him gone, merely returned to Paris.

Burtzev could not in this instance, as he did in many others, publicly announce the exposure without compromising his mail intercept practices. But he depended on the revolutionary groups in which Kuryansky and Poznansky worked as Okhrana agents to proceed with exposure and liquidation. An Okhrana agent in Burtzev's service had learned about his trip on the day he arrived in London, too late to alert Kuryansky. Kuryansky was dismissed with three months' pay and left England, but soon thereafter the revolutionaries found him in France and carried out the death sentence of their underground tribunal.

The Smolyansky Case

Burtzev could not disregard the judgments of Mark Natanson, who as a member of the Central Committee was the channel for the funds he required. Although he often forced Natanson to yield to him—even in some cases where his own intelligence was incorrect—Natanson's independent investigations sometimes complicated his efforts. Natanson was practical and rational in his approach, whereas Burtzev, relying heavily on his analysis of recorded data, was impulsive and too sure of his own intuition.

One case in which Burtzev was completely wrong was that of a revolutionary activist named Smolyansky. In falsely accusing him of being an Okhrana agent, he built his case entirely on circumstantial evidence. This included the suspect's intercepted mail and letters from accusers, anonymous and signed. His income was unexplained, and his movements were suspicious. One of his purloined writings was about the Party of Socialist Revolutionaries, and Burtzev saw this as clearly the draft for an agent report. Then Burtzev received a report that a brother of Smolyansky's was a police official in Russia. He regarded the evidence as sufficient to warrant exposing the man as an agent.

Natanson objected. He had made an extensive investigation himself, and the results were quite contrary to the allegations in Burtzev's brief. He argued that the Smolyanskys were Jews and so could

93

not be employed as police officials anywhere in Russia. Smolyansky was well versed in the affairs of the party, but his way of life and his activities among the émigrés precluded the possibility of his being a police agent. Burtzev then renewed his investigations and gathered still more evidence to support his accusation. He won in the end by appealing to the comrades not to trust anyone. They had trusted people in the past who proved to be traitors, he argued, and that must not occur again.

Tsipin

On the other hand, Burtzev was right and Natanson wrong about an Okhrana agent named Tsipin, who lived lavishly with his wife in a Paris suburb. Natanson's queries in Petersburg seemed to confirm Tsipin's loyalty to the cause. The reports from Russia said that he had been helpful to the party in the capital even before he joined and that he had since distinguished himself as a trustworthy activist. He was described as the son of a well-to-do merchant, who should therefore have money enough to live comfortably abroad.

Burtzev was not satisfied with Natanson's findings. He sought help from the wife of the Socialist Revolutionary leader Viktor Lebedev, pen name Voronov, who lived in the same suburb as the Tsipins. When the two women were visiting one day, Mme. Tsipin displayed a number of picture postcards she and her husband had received from Petersburg. Mme. Lebedev was interested in more than the pictures; she was curious about the names of the writers. She asked questions about them for which Mme. Tsipin had no ready answers. During further chatting, Mme. Lebedev wondered whether her friend couldn't keep her husband from his careless squandering of money; this turned the talk to incomes. Mme. Lebedev, protesting that it was none of her business, nevertheless pointed out discrepancies for which Mme. Tsipin could give no logical explanation. A full account of the questions and answers went to Burtzev, who in the meantime had gathered further information that added to his doubts.

Burtzev's demand for a direct questioning of Tsipin was approved by Natanson, provided, however, that it should take the form of a friendly conversation. Lebedev and Stepan Sletov, both on good terms with the suspect, were entrusted with the disguised probing; it was hoped that they would turn up some lead for further investigation. But Tsipin, as if sensing the purpose of the talks, had a ready answer for everything. This increased suspicion but provided no proof

94

Sherlock Holmes

on the basis of which he could be denounced as a police agent. In a secret meeting it was therefore decided that he should not be permitted access to any gatherings of the party; the revolutionaries should break all contact with him. The case was terminated on 24 January 1913 with an announcement of Tsipin's suicide. He was said to have shot himself on the train between Paris and Versailles.

Tatiana Tsetlin

Burtzev's exposure of Okhrana agent Tatiana Tsetlin, pseudonym Maria Tsikhotskaïa, was preceded by a long investigation of the circumstances leading to failures in the conspiracies in which she participated. She had joined the Okhrana at Petersburg in 1907 and been placed as a penetration agent in the Socialist Revolutionaries' Combat Unit. The Petersburg police soon arrested most members of that unit but not Tatiana. She went to Geneva and joined another Combat Unit, which assigned her in the fall of 1908 to a team being organized by a Paris comrade, Josif Minor, to go to Petersburg and kill the Tsar. Minor left for Russia ahead of the others in order to make advance preparations; he was arrested upon arrival.

Tatiana remained in Paris associated with Boris Savinkov, the new leader of the Combat Unit, who formed a team with her and two others to begin by killing General Gerasimov of the Gendarmes and an Okhrana headquarters official named Dobroskokov. This was in March 1909. Dobroskokov, it happened, was a good friend of Tatiana's. Only two months before that date he had sent her a package of books through the cover address of an agent named Kershner. She now sent a wire to Petersburg asking him to come to Paris without delay because his life was in danger. Dobroskokov did so, arriving in Paris on Good Friday. The only ones who knew about his trip were General Gerasimov and his assistant in Petersburg and agent Kershner in Paris.

Burtzev had been watching Tatiana. He had studied the circumstances of her unhindered departure from Petersburg in 1907 after most of her comrades were arrested. He had compiled notes on Minor's arrest at the end of a trip which only she and two or three others knew about. He now learned of Dobroskokov's surprise journey just after being chosen as the victim of an assassination plan known only to Tatiana's team. He quickly organized an exceptionally large surveillance team to cover Dobroskokov and his contacts in Paris.

95

Sherlock Holmes

As Dobroskokov stepped off the train he immediately noticed three revolutionary agents and even recognized one of them; but he and Kershner, who met him, could detect no surveillance. When Tatiana came to visit him the following day, however, it became obvious that the revolutionaries had followed her. On her return home she found a telegram from Savinkov asking her to come on 13 April to the apartment of Sinkovsky, a member of her terrorist team. When she did so she was received by ten terrorists and Savinkov, who held a pistol on her.

Revolutionary Justice

The manner of Tatiana's arrest, interrogation, and trial by the underground tribunal is typical of the procedures used in cases of accused traitors. Savinkov ordered her to raise her arms and kept the pistol at her temple while she was being searched. He took from her all her money and told her that 500 rubles found in her apartment had also been confiscated as belonging to the party because it came from the Russian government. Sinkovsky, also a suspect, was being held in an adjoining room.

Tatiana had been under suspicion and investigation, she learned, for half a year, since the fall of 1908. The revolutionaries were familiar with the quarters of Dobroskokov at Petersburg; they had investigated there. They had also penetrated a safe house and learned there the code names of both Tatiana and Sinkovsky. They knew the true name of agent Kershner and the fact that Tatiana had received books through him from Petersburg.

Tatiana and Sinkovsky in the adjoining room were held for five days, watched by up to seven or eight armed members of the Combat Unit. On the second morning there arrived five members of the revolutionary tribunal and a recording secretary. The salient figure at the trial, not acting as one of the judges, was Burtzev with his intelligence records and incriminating papers picked up in the search of Tatiana's quarters, including a number of notes in Dobroskokov's handwriting.

After Burtzev's statement of the case, the tribunal began a long cross examination. Tatiana denied nothing. She declared that she had served the Okhrana but insisted that Sinkovsky had never been a police agent. She admitted acting as a secret agent for two years and made no effort to embellish her position before the court.

96

Sherlock Holmes

The tribunal decided that she was an "unrepenting provocateur" and sentenced both her and Sinkovsky to death.

The two prisoners were kept in the apartment waiting to be killed. The guards were changed constantly, at times seven, never fewer than three, all armed. Altogether, Tatiana estimated, some thirty people came and left the building. The landlord's attention was attracted by the great commotion. On 19 April, without explanation, both prisoners were told the death sentence was commuted. The revolutionaries had apparently decided it would be too dangerous to carry out the execution: too many people knew about the trial and the concierge had seen too much; the liquidation could be done later, away from Paris. The prisoners were told that they were expelled from the party but would have to report all changes of address. Both were released.

Tatiana was given back 40 francs of her money. She took a train to Germany. Three armed revolutionaries accompanied her, but she succeeded in escaping from them. She returned to Russia and told the Okhrana this story.

Burtzev as Interrogator

Burtzev himself, in contrast to the others, refrained from pistol threats and abusive language when interrogating. In the case of agent Aleksandr Maas, for instance, he had piled up ample evidence of treason. But in a series of interrogations after his accusation and before the final sitting of the tribunal he, the accuser, acted more gently than even Maas's friends who were serving as judges. Talking like a kindly old professor, he began by apologizing to Maas that the interrogation had to be held because of some reports received from Petersburg. But behind this apparently timid handling was a systematic strategy to prove that the man was lying. Burtzev encouraged Maas to develop a fictitious story about his income. The story became so extensive and elaborate as to provide many facets subject to factual checking, and the traitor was caught in his own fiction.

We have seen Burtzev's ingenuity in eliciting information from the unwilling Okhrana ex-director Lopukhin. In another case, when an underground tribunal had decided to dispatch a team to kill Okhrana penetration Zinaida Zhuchenko, Burtzev first rushed to her apartment for a talk. Assuring her that he would save her life, he gently developed a lengthy interrogation, avoiding arguments, giving advice, and astutely probing into her past activities. She did not believe his as-

97

   *Sherlock Holmes*

surances, but she could not refuse to answer his kindly and considerate questions. She gave him the story of her long service for the Okhrana, trying nevertheless to reveal nothing that could give clues to the service's current operations.

CI Hybris

After Burtzev's triumph in exposing Azev and Harting, no revolutionary group was able to refuse his services or to ignore his warnings and directives. The central committees had to accept him in their councils and consult him on the security of projected operations and the loyalty of participating activists. Thus he acquired a peculiar authority over revolutionary operations and the top party leaders. He was frequently able to tell them to change or drop their operational plans.

After Natanson and Chernov, for example, had in 1913 approved a project to dispatch Ziama Kisin with a team to Petersburg to murder Minister of Education Kaso, Burtzev warned them that the conspiracy might have been penetrated by the Okhrana. When they wanted to go ahead with the operation despite his warnings, he threatened to expose them as provocateurs if anything should go wrong. They had to drop the plan. We have seen how in the Smolyansky case Burtzev was entirely wrong, yet Natanson and the other top leaders could not contradict him. He had only to remind them, "For five years I worked on Azev and proved him to be an agent, but the comrades refused to listen," and the central committees were compelled to follow his dicta.

His authoritarian attitude led to a gradual loss of support from the Socialist Revolutionaries and other groups of political exiles. He became chronically short of the funds required to maintain his expanded services. Bakai, after he broke with him, wrote him a public letter in which he charged him with squandering money:

> Despite abundant income you have found yourself financially embarrassed at all times. And you have driven to a financially critical position all, including myself, who had the misfortune of having had dealings with you.

Burtzev may have been a poor financial manager; certainly he was more secretive with regard to funds than any other operational matter. The Okhrana's penetration agents learned and reported virtually every operational plan and action undertaken by his service, but they were never able to render a comprehensive report on where his money

98

came from and how it was spent. Toward the end, at least, it seems clear that his subsidies simply fell off.

The negative side of Burtzev's activities came in for ever sharper criticism. Some of the revolutionary comrades saw in him an evil spirit doing more damage than good to the revolution. His fanatical drive to uncover Okhrana penetration agents at home and abroad created an atmosphere of fear and suspicion among the rank and file. His callous accusations of treason often turned out to be based on insufficient information and hasty assumptions. Two of the Russians in the original "Leroy Brigade," for example, were wrongly accused and committed suicide.

Then some whom Burtzev brought to trial by the underground tribunals cleared themselves as innocent, occasionally even when he was right, and he was obliged to recant with public apology. Sometimes his intemperate charges and subsequent retractions actually helped Okhrana agents, for example Emil Brontman and his mistress Eropkina, to establish themselves more firmly than ever in the revolutionary councils. At the same time accusations against innocents compelled many to desert the movement.

The Fall

Opposition to Burtzev increased particularly in the first months of 1914. Rumors were spread to show him full of naiveté or senile. He was called an old autocrat who conjured up suspects by intuition, without factual intelligence information and proof. He was charged with an obsession for exposing police agents regardless of how much he hurt the revolutionary movement.

With a new series of errors in exposing Okhrana agents the criticism came to a head in mid-1914, and Burtzev lost all financial support from the revolutionary groups. His teams of French external agents disintegrated because their salaries were not paid, and his wide circle of Russian collaborators gradually deserted him. By the time the war broke out in August he was actually destitute, without support from anywhere and thus without a service. He returned to Russia, escaping a throng of creditors to face in the imperial courts the charges of sedition against him. He made assertions that he did not want to oppose a government allied with the democratic West in a war against German militarism; but the true cause for his return appears to have been his loss of supporters among the revolutionaries and his consequent bankruptcy.

99

There had been times when Vladimir Lvovich had been wanted dead or alive by the Tsarist regime. Returning to Petrograd in wartime, however, he found the authorities unexpectedly lenient. A free man even before the first revolution broke out, he went back to newspaper work in 1917, publishing *Obshchee Delo* (Common Cause). He now became an ardent critic of Bolshevism. Despite his many past services for Lenin's party, therefore, he found it healthiest to return to exile soon after the October Revolution. In Paris he continued his *Obshchee Delo* for several years. His death came in 1942 at the age of 80.

100

CONFIDENTIAL

Gambler against the Russian revolutionaries and wartime double agent with the Germans.

OKHRANA AGENT DOLIN [1]

Rita T. Kronenbitter

The provincial branch chiefs of the imperial Okhrana were not required in 1904 to report to St. Petersburg the names and assignments of their informants and secret agents. Only in very exceptional cases did they seek headquarters' advice about some outstanding agent. One such case was that of Ventsion Moiseev-Moshkov Dolin (pronounced *Dallin*). Young Dolin, who had a four years' record of good work as agent and informer but had been on ice for several months, came one day in June that year to his former case officer wanting to be put in prison. What he really wanted, of course, was reemployment; a duly advertised arrest was the almost standard procedure for building cover. The case officer, Captain Shultz, newly appointed chief of the Okhrana branch in Ekaterinoslav (Dnepropetrovsk), was undecided whether to comply.

Dolin had started as an informer in 1900 while going to school in Zhitomir, west of Kiev. He had worked there for a Colonel Potocki for two years. Potocki had recommended him to Shultz as intelligent and experienced in maintaining effective contacts among the underground leaders of the Jewish Bund, citing a whole series of subversive acts he had been able to prevent thanks to Dolin's timely information. Shultz had soon found for himself how good a man he was, raised his status to that of secret—penetration—agent, and paid him 100 rubles a month, more than any other agent in the area.

Dolin had one serious defect, however, which had been the reason for his dismissal and was why Captain Shultz now consulted headquarters about rehiring him: he was a passionate and incorrigible gambler. Although Shultz had previously warned him that he would have to live modestly and give up gambling, another agent had

---

[1] This case history is reconstructed principally from files of the Tsarist agency's Paris field station, which the Hoover Institution has now opened to the public. For earlier papers by the author from this source see *Studies* IX 2 and 3, "The Okhrana's Female Agents," Parts I and II.

4. *(Continued)*

reported watching Bundist agitator Dolin—neither knew the other was an agent—lose heavily at dice at the town club and hearing his comrades speculate about where he got his money. This was just after several subversives close to Dolin had been arrested and people were wondering who betrayed them. So Captain Shultz had felt obliged to dismiss him. He told him to break off with the Bund and go back home to Ostropol, over by Rovno, where his father had a small business.

Applying now for reemployment, Dolin presented his own plan for his future activity. Having had no contact with the Bund for several months, he would formally join the Anarcho-Communists this time; he had already made a number of friends among them. He proposed that after being arrested he should be sent back to Zhitomir for trial and imprisonment so as to make his defiance of the police better known and admired among the subversives. Shultz passed this buck to headquarters, received a go-ahead, worked out the details with Dolin, and proceeded as planned. The agent was taken to Zhitomir and sentenced for certain political offenses someone else had committed.

Counter-terror in the Ukraine

Upon release from prison, Dolin was promptly welcomed into the terrorist underground. He moved back to Ekaterinoslav, which had become an Anarcho-Communist center and transit point for the terrorists. There a series of conspiracies for assassinations and sabotage were nipped short of the point of action as he succeeded in learning of the plans and reporting the movements of underground personnel. Early in 1908 the Okhrana provincial branches were alerted by headquarters against a Jewess named Taratuta, who had taken part in several killings of high officials. Dolin told his case officer, now a Captain Prutensky, that he could finger her for arrest, but it should be worth a bonus of 500 rubles. Headquarters readily approved Prutensky's borrowing the money for this purpose, and Dolin signed a receipt for it in his code name, *Lenin.* Taking extreme care to make it look like a lucky accident, Prutensky bagged Taratuta along with several other conspirators. Dolin himself was among the group, but there seemed to be no evidence to incriminate him this time.

To take off him any possible heat generated by his release, however, Captain Prutensky in August sent Dolin on an exploratory trip to Paris. He knew that the revolutionaries in his Ekaterinoslav area

4. *(Continued)*

were receiving funds, arms, and guidance from their comrades in France, and he wanted to look into the workings of this supply and communications line. In Paris, Dolin characteristically wired for money: for 400 rubles he could produce the mailing list of the *Burevestnik*, underground publication of the Anarcho-Communists. Prutensky, always short of cash, consulted headquarters and was told it had no interest in a list of Anarcho-Communists abroad but he should offer 200 rubles for the list of those in Russia.

Dolin arrived back in Ekaterinoslav early in September, bringing the mailing list. With its help he was able to spot for his case officer the location of two Burevestnik printshops in Russia, several caches of propaganda materials and hidden arms depots, and a detailed plan for the transport of activists and literature into the country. So comprehensive was this information that Prutensky wired for the Police Director's approval for him to bring Dolin to St. Petersburg to discuss it. It affected Okhrana branches all over the Empire, and he realized that such a productive agent should be reporting to headquarters, not his provincial branch at Ekaterinoslav. Headquarters, he suggested, should give Dolin a permanent assignment abroad as a penetration agent.

It happened that the Paris station needed a replacement for its penetration agent among the Anarcho-Communists, a man named Tetelbaum, code name *Yost*, who just a few months earlier had been exposed and killed. Klimovich, the Police Director, was agreeable to Dolin's transfer but wired Prutensky that it should be cleared with station chief Arkady Harting at rue de Grenelle 79, Paris, and gave instructions for secure communication direct with him. The transfer was thus agreed upon, with the provision that Prutensky could retain Dolin in Ekaterinoslav until the end of September for a special job.

Bad Rubles for Good

This job was to locate 8,000 rubles which a combat unit of the Anarcho-Communists had recently "expropriated" from the local state treasury. Dolin learned that the loot had been smuggled to Geneva, and Captain Prutensky promptly sent him there, wiring Harting in Paris in order at the same time to effect the agent's transfer. Harting expressed his delight at having *Lenin* and dispatched his case officer Captain Andreev to Geneva.

Dolin, established in the Geneva group of Anarcho-Communists, attended an underground gathering where they discussed the use of

4. *(Continued)*

the 8,000 rubles. 3,000 of the total was to be allocated back to the Odessa underground to cover the expenses of an operation up the Dniester in Khotin. The plan of. this operation was to smuggle in a pile of counterfeit money, 49,000 rubles, and exchange it for genuine banknotes from the state treasury in Khotin with the help of the chief accountant there. As usual in selecting operatives for such risky tasks, the conspirators cast dice, and Dolin won.

He reported the assignment to Captain Andreev, explaining that he could not possibly turn it down. He was to leave on 17 November for Kolomiya in Austrian Galicia, on the border only some 100 kilometers from Khotin. There an elderly woman named Steora Ivanchuk at 90 Starogoncharska had the 49,000 counterfeit rubles in safekeeping. From Kolomiya he was to proceed to Odessa, arriving 21 November, to coordinate with the local underground. There, Captain Andreev now instructed him, he should also contact a Lt. Col. Levdikov, responsible for Okhrana activities in Khotin. Upon receiving the spurious money he would note the serial numbers and report. Case officer and agent discussed the job in minute detail, and Paris spelled out all their arrangements in wires to St. Petersburg.

The operation turned out a complete success for the Okhrana. Chief accountant Malaidach and Anarchist Dudnichko were caught red-handed, ostensibly quite by accident and without a trace of suspicion falling on Dolin, who returned to Geneva on 20 December. Captain Andreev debriefed him there and wired to headquarters the following account:

> Arriving in Khotin from Odessa, Lenin contacted through local Anarcho-Communists the accountant of the state treasury and gave him 3,000 rubles of the money taken in the robbery of the Ekaterinoslav state treasury. The accountant agreed to take 16,000 in counterfeit bills in exchange for genuine money. Lenin then returned to Kolomiya in Austria to pick up the 16,000. He came back and delivered the counterfeit notes to a go-between for the accountant, who was promptly taken under surveillance by the agents of the Odessa Branch. Lenin also gave to Lt. Colonel Levdikov a complete list of the Anarcho-Communist group in Khotin. Nine were arrested and much illegal literature confiscated. Lenin returned to Geneva. He was given a reward of 400 rubles.

A year later, in November of 1909, Dolin asked for assignment to Odessa, saying he didn't get along with the Anarcho-Communists in Paris. By the middle of the month the Odessa Okhrana had enough information from *Aleksandrov* (his new code name) to arrest the entire Anarcho-Communist underground there. To play safe,

4. *(Continued)*

however, they included him among the arrested. Dolin himself maintained that he was not under suspicion in connection with these arrests, that the terrorists were convinced another person was the traitor; but he acceded to his case officer's insistence. The case officer promised that at a convenient spot he would be given an opportunity to escape, along with several other prisoners.

The branch chief overruled this plan. An easy escape, even in a group with others, might cause suspicion. Dolin had become too valuable to expose to unnecessary danger. It would be safer to send him with the rest into banishment. On 21 January 1910 he was thus shipped with other exiles to Archangelsk. Soon thereafter he received 500 rubles and a passport in the name of Gregory Solomonovich Gleichsberg. At the end of May he "escaped" to St. Petersburg; a month later he reported in at Odessa. He paid a short visit to his parents, now nearby in Kherson.

Third Start

In July Dolin's case officer supplied him with a passport in the name of Heim Yankel Eisenberg, issued by the Odessa municipal government, and he made an "illegal escape" abroad. He went to Paris, where A. A. Krassilnikov was now in charge and a Colonel Erhardt became Dolin's case officer. He was given the code name *Sharl* (Charles) and placed in Switzerland. Within two months he asked for 2,000 francs, saying he needed it to pay his debts. Erhardt supported the request in a wire to headquarters: "I saw Sharl and he made a very good impression. He is genuine and conscientious. As a penetration among the Anarcho-Communists he is very close to Muzil, Muzil's wife, and others. I value him greatly and recommend approval."

Dolin's salary in Switzerland was 650 francs a month, plus expenses for trips to Paris and London to visit the Anarcho-Communist groups there. Although his operations during this prewar period never included such risky assignments as those in Russia before 1910, the value of his work was never questioned. In one instance he played a curious role in fixing the blame for some arrests he himself had arranged upon the Anarcho-Communists' own chief underground operator.

This was the case of the above-named Muzil, whose life career was that of a terrorist for the Anarcho-Communists. A Czech, at the turn of the century he had organized various bands in the Balkan countries in support of the Russian revolutionaries. Then he had worked in Galicia and the Prussian parts of Poland as an organizer of border crossings. By 1911 he had moved to London and become a member of the committee of the Anarcho-Communists there. Despite his great services in the past, he came under suspicion as a traitor when it was pointed out that his arrival from Galicia had coincided with the arrest of a whole net of conspirators entering Russia from that province.

The revolutionaries' counterintelligence service in Paris, run by the sometimes overzealous Burtzev, produced information which incriminated Muzil further, so the Anarcho-Communists were obliged to subject him to interrogation and judgment before a secret tribunal. Dolin had by then gained the confidence of the comrades to such a degree that they entrusted him with the investigation and membership on the tribunal. He succeeded in confirming Burtzev's charges and branding Muzil an agent of the Okhrana, thus eliminating him—although vindicated after the revolution as a faithful terrorist—from further conspiratorial work.

Dolin remained in London as one of the leading Anarcho-Communists until 1914, making occasional trips to Switzerland and reporting regularly on the revolutionaries' projects. When the war broke out he wanted to return to Russia, but a sudden opportunity to join the German service as a double agent for the Okhrana launched him on a new career, hitherto little known though one of the Okhrana's most dramatic. The revolutionary writers who have traced his work as a penetration agent among their ranks break off in 1914, purposely omitting his contribution to the Russian national war effort against Germany. His extraordinary achievements in misleading the German service, exposing it, and doing it material damage did not fit into their portrayal of him as a traitor. They only note in conclusion that he committed suicide in Russia when the Communists took over. And that, Valerian Agafonov declares in his book, was too good an end for him.

Bid from Byzantium

The beginnings of Dolin's new venture show up in a number of priority cables exchanged at the end of September 1914 between station chief Krassilnikov in Paris and headquarters. Dolin had attended an underground meeting of the Anarcho-Communists in Switzerland, and afterwards a visiting revolutionary comrade from

4. *(Continued)*

Constantinople had introduced himself to him. His name was Bernstein, he said, and he was fully informed of Dolin's great revolutionary merits; a brother in Milan had told him where to find him.

Bernstein had been commissioned by the Turkish government, he said, to recruit a team of revolutionaries to go to Russia and commit three acts of sabotage there. The Turks would pay big money and provide all the required equipment. Targets would be two strategic bridges in central Russia and one in Siberia. Technical details, including the pinpointing of the targets, were to be worked out in Constantinople. There would be a liberal advance allowance, and a 50,000-franc reward would be deposited in a bank. If Dolin was willing to undertake the job, he could select one or two other revolutionaries to go with him to Constantinople to organize the expedition.

Dolin responded favorably with a studied mixture of enthusiasm and caution. He agreed to look for a partner, preferably not Jewish but a fully trusted Russian. Then he reported to Colonel Erhardt, who rushed with the story to chief Krassilnikov. A venture like this had to be approved at headquarters, if only because the Okhrana was supposed to confine itself to work against the revolutionaries. Should Dolin see Bernstein again or not? Should he explore the possibilities of a double-agent operation? Should he go to Constantinople and thence to Russia? Who should be designated to go with him?

The director's reply favored the operation. Dolin should continue the talks and agree to go to Turkey and then Russia. No agent working among the revolutionaries should be made a member of the sabotage team; Dolin's aide should be a staff officer. The two should travel separately to Constantinople, never recognizing each other in public and taking utmost care against possible Turkish surveillance. Their correspondence back should be in secret inks agreed on in advance and signed with female names. If the time and location for entering Russia could not be reported in advance, Dolin should upon arrival wire Vassiliev at 40 Nadezhdinskaia, so that secure contacts could be arranged and the movement of the team watched. Krassilnikov should keep headquarters informed in detail on the operation, including membership of the sabotage team. Could Dolin pick whom he wanted or would the decision be made in Constantinople?

Krassilnikov designated Colonel Erhardt to pose as Dolin's assistant. Erhardt insisted on changing the location for further talks with

4. *(Continued)*

Bernstein from Venice, the rendezvous agreed upon, to Rome. It was 4 November before the three met there. Dolin introduced Erhardt as "Tovarishch Mikhail, our chief organizer," and asked Bernstein to repeat his whole proposition to him. Bernstein revealed his disappointment that after this long wait Dolin had not brought the rest of the team so they could all proceed to Constantinople without delay. On the other hand, he was evidently glad for the chance to discuss with a top revolutionary leader further sabotage possibilities that he could propose to his bosses in Constantinople. He thus showed himself to be more than just a spotter and recruiter; in the four days of meetings that followed, he developed all sorts of ideas on likely sabotage targets. He also showed whom he was working for.

The German Hand

Colonel Erhardt had never believed that Bernstein's backers were the Turks, but he did not ask any direct questions. The story came out piecemeal. Bernstein was a civilian supplier for the German military in Constantinople and had much business in the embassy. One of the officials there had asked him to get in touch with the Russian revolutionaries to arrange the blowing up of the bridges on the Volga at Syzrani, on the Yenissei near Krasnoyarsk, and on the railroad line circling Lake Baikal, 50,000 francs to be paid upon completion of the three jobs. That was why he was here. Although he had kept moving while waiting in Italy—as a subject of Turkey, he did not want to attract the attention of the local police—he was nevertheless in steady communication with the German who sent him, and this man was getting impatient.

In the course of the talks Colonel Erhardt let it be seen that he was the one in charge but Dolin was the man to lead the sabotage team. "Why did you say at first that the Turks were behind this proposal? I would like to hear your explanation," the colonel challenged Bernstein. "As an organizer and planner for the revolutionaries, I insist on utmost frankness. We must know where we stand and whose support we can count on." Bernstein explained that he had to mask the offer until he was sure it would be accepted. Now he would be completely frank. The next thing for the three of them to do was to go to Constantinople.

Colonel Erhardt declined to go; his past revolutionary activities had so compromised him in the Balkans, he said, that his mere appearance there would endanger the project. Moreover, he needed to go

4. *(Continued)*

to London to get comrades not only for the three bridge jobs but for the other operations Bernstein's sponsor was anxious to undertake. He had already alerted four persons in London to wait for his personal instructions. As soon as he got there he would send an assistant to Italy to join Dolin for the trip to Constantinople and would also organize a separate sabotage team to be sent to Russia by the northern route; upon arrival in the Empire that team could coordinate its activity with Dolin and his comrade entering direct from Turkey. Thus Bernstein was consoled for the delay by the prospect of an additional sabotage expedition from London.

Before the Rome talks were over the planning was suddenly complicated by Turkey's entering the war on the German side. This would make it impossible to ship the sabotage explosives in from Turkey as planned. Erhardt assured Bernstein that they need not worry about this. The explosives could be procured in Russia; the organized workers at the Yuzovka ammunition plant could be depended upon to provide whatever materials and technicians were needed. On the other hand, it would now be extremely unwise for the Russians to go to Constantinople. The talks with the German boss should therefore be held on neutral soil, say in Salonika.

Bernstein objected that the German official was such an important person that his traveling to Salonika would draw too much attention. He said he had already wired the German embassy to send to the consul at Salonika four German and Turkish passports for the Russians. There should be no problem in visiting Constantinople, he insisted, for the Germans had become the real bosses in Turkey. They left this point open but agreed on immediate moves: Bernstein would go to Brindisi to buy three steamship tickets for Salonika; Dolin would wait in Rome for the arrival of his assistant and the two would join Bernstein in Brindisi; Erhardt would proceed to London to organize the other sabotage team. Bernstein promised to send two thousand pounds for the expenses of this team. Its targets would be three arms plants, the most important of which was one at Bryansk operated by French capital. Awards for these sabotage acts would be decided upon between Dolin and the German.

For his expenses on the return trip to London Bernstein gave Colonel Erhardt 300 francs. Submitting his progress report to Krassilnikov in Paris, the colonel attached the banknotes with the comment that he considered them Okhrana property. The large amounts that Dolin was later to get from the Germans would similarly revert to

4. *(Continued)*

the Paris station. even when for the sake of cover Dolin had to make deposits in his name.

Mission Accomplished

From this point on, action on the part of the Okhrana was rapid. Before returning to Paris to report to Krassilnikov, Colonel Erhardt stopped in Genoa and briefed the case officer, Lt. Colonel Anton Litvin, whom Krassilnikov had dispatched to join Dolin. In Paris he sent a wire to Salonika for delivery to Litvin and Dolin upon arrival saying they should under no circumstances agree to go to Constantinople; the Turks could arrest the conspirators as Russian subjects. Bernstein must persuade the German officer to come to Greece, or the deal would be called off.

Erhardt sent another wire to headquarters asking for operational support: Dolin needed an address in Russia for correspondence with Bernstein; he needed documents that would enable him to move freely in any part of the Empire; around the end of December a newspaper in the capital should carry an item about the criminal sabotage of a railroad bridge without specifying the location. "Since the German embassy in Turkey appears extremely anxious to conceal its initiation and funding of the operations," he wrote, "it would be desirable to have a subsequent news item report that two criminals had been arrested but others could not be found." As in other communications with headquarters, he begged in this one for the utmost in security precautions. Dolin's "movements must be watched at all times and contacts with him maintained in complete clandestinity. This good man has given more than ten years of excellent service with extraordinary achievement. To protect him from exposure must be our heavy personal responsibility."

Litvin arrived in Rome on 9 November and was introduced to Bernstein as Tovarishch Anatoly, operational assistant of Tovarishch Mikhail (Erhardt) and an experienced revolutionary terrorist. The three boarded ship in Brindisi separately and had no open contact with one another on the way. In Salonika, they had no difficulty persuading the German sponsor that they could not go to Constantinople; he agreed to meet them in still neutral Rumania.

The briefing in Bucharest took only two days. Dolin and his partner, it was arranged, would enter Russia from Rumania. The German furnished them passports, Dolin's in the name of René Ralph and Litvin's as Anatoly Linden. He gave them money for travel,

66

4. *(Continued)*

supplies, and the pay of revolutionary helpers. To Dolin he gave another ten thousand francs to send to "Tovarishch Mikhail" for the northern team. Dolin was to be the sole channel for communication with Bernstein about both teams' operations, and the German control and direction would likewise all be channeled through Bernstein.

The Okhrana control was, naturally, more complex. Headquarters designated one of its top officials, code name *Orlov*, to run the operation in Russia and coordinate with the elements abroad—Krassilnikov in Bordeaux (where the field station had moved on account of the German threat to Paris), Colonel Erhardt with code name *Shpeer* for this operation, the notional group of revolutionary saboteurs in London, and of course Bernstein in Constantinople as the recipient of Dolin's communications. It was *Orlov*, then, that arranged for real but harmless acts of sabotage, saw to it that vague and exaggerated reports of them appeared in the press, and made sure they were leaked to foreign newspapers. Several Paris papers carried short items about dastardly bombings of installations in Russia, complete with dates and worded to suggest truly serious damage.

Emptor Cavet

The German service seemed convinced and gratified by the accomplishments of the sabotage teams in Russia. But when Dolin came back out in March, ostensibly with Litvin (who actually had not stayed in Russia at all), they were instructed through Bernstein to go to Bern to see the German military attaché, Colonel von Bismarck. This officer met with them twice, hearing full reports on how they had sabotaged two bridges and planted a bomb in the Okhta armament factory; and as they were telling him about this last act, he interrupted them angrily:

"That Okhta incident was not sabotage. It was not an explosion intended to do any damage. You are both liars."

When the two protested, Bismarck revealed he had another source of information in Russia who had reported that the Okhta explosion was clearly staged so as to cause no damage to life or property. But Dolin and Litvin stuck to their story, so the attaché promised he would consult his home office for further explanation and a decision on whether to continue the operation. He said he would send for them when he had an answer from Berlin.

Several weeks went by with no word from Bismarck. When Dolin and Litvin then insisted on seeing him again anyway, he said that since there had been no reply from Berlin he had no choice but to dismiss them. Again he accused them of not being genuinely interested in the work but only wanting to make some dishonest money. When Litvin realized that the German had no suspicion of their double game but only of mercenary rascalry, he swelled with feigned anger and disgust, exploding: "You can keep your money; we want no part of it! You can't buy our services. We are revolutionaries! We aren't here to help you or get your pay. What we want is to strike against the tyranny in our country!" Dolin seconded the short speech with convincing vigor.

This act so impressed Colonel von Bismarck that his attitude immediately changed to one of apology. He told them he would send another wire to Berlin at once. In a few days, on 12 June 1915, he invited them to his villa and told them his headquarters had approved resuming the operation. He introduced them to a man he called Franklin A. Giacomini who would thenceforth work with them. Giacomini claimed to be an American citizen who was in sympathy with the German war effort; that was why the German government had asked him to deal with them.

Litvin, as he later reported to headquarters, quickly saw through this purported American. What would an American be doing in the villa of the German military attaché? The man's posture, walk, and general manner showed he must be another German officer.

The three now held a series of meetings without Bismarck. Giacomini said he was going to Petrograd—as an American citizen, he could—and was anxious to meet the revolutionary employee of the Okhta plant who had taken part in sabotaging it. Dolin and Litvin, realizing at once that the object was to check up on their story, said they did not know the man but were sure his name could be obtained from a Dr. Naum Borisovich Liakhovsky at 35 Nevsky, who was an expert in explosives and a trusted revolutionary. Begging Giacomini to be careful not to give the doctor away, they said he could give him their names as "Rekord" and "Ralph" and certify to their concurrence in the inquiry into the factory job.

To the second meeting, on 14 June, Giacomini brought a check for 10,000 francs against the Reichsbank account in the Swiss Federal Bank. He told Dolin to be careful with this money; it was for expenses in several forthcoming operations. One of these was to explode a bomb in the residence of Russian Minister Sazonov; another bomb was to be planted in the Putilov ammunition works; and several

58

Okhrana Agent

were to be set off in coal mines in the Donets basin. Giacomini asked Dolin to prepare a list of strategic locations where he would recommend other acts of sabotage.

At the last meeting before Giacomini's departure, Dolin and Litvin briefed him on procedure and passwords for making contact with Dr. Liakhovsky. Litvin himself would go to Petrograd and would be staying at the Severnaia Hotel in case he was needed. After the meeting Litvin wired headquarters Giacomini's personal description, his expected arrival date of 28 or 29 June, and the information that he was as familiar as a native with Petrograd. The Dr. Liakhovsky he would contact was of course an Okhrana agent, but not knowing how far the Okhrana directorate would want to carry the game with him, Litvin requested that an agent be placed in the Okhta plant to pose as the revolutionary who had helped sabotage it.

More Dastardly Bombs

Dolin deposited the check for projected operations in the Russian Asian Bank in Zurich and left for Paris. Here it was agreed that he would join Litvin in London and accompany him back to Russia. Then headquarters, oddly, objected to his going back in on the German assignments. Wires were bounded back and forth, Krassilnikov insisting he must go lest he be blown to the Germans, and also to the revolutionaries through Bernstein. In the end he was in Petrograd again by the middle of July.

Dolin's job was quite simple this time. He only had to brief a headquarters case officer on everything the Germans had instructed him to do and let the Okhrana stage the explosions or otherwise simulate the sabotage. A bomb exploded in the mansion of Minister Sazonov, just as the Germans had prescribed. It was no dud, but it was used in such a way as to cause minimal damage to the property. In sequel, the Okhrana directorate cabled to the chief in Paris:

> Find ways in the French press, without revealing source, to publish the following note: "A large bomb exploded in the mansion of one of the chiefs of the Ministry of Foreign Affairs. One servant received wounds and a section of the mansion is in ruins. The perpetrator escaped."
>
> Put varied versions of this item in different newspapers.

A similar cable eight days later gave the text for a news item about a bomb explosion in one of the major mines of the Donets coal basin. It said the damage would stop production for a considerable length of time, that several people had been arrested, and that the

4. *(Continued)*

authorities were conducting a thorough investigation. Another dated 8 August requested a story in the French press of how an armed man simulating insanity broke into the Bureau of Foreign Affairs intending to kill the Minister. Only the Deputy, Neratov, was present, and employees overpowered and disarmed the assassin. Investigation proved that a group of conspirators was behind the attempt. Paris Okhrana was not to discuss this with the ambassador; it was a planned incident essential in *Sharl's* operation.

Publicity for acts of sabotage and attempted assassinations stretched on through several months of 1915. Each simulated incident had to be realistic enough to convince any German observer on the spot. But Franklin Giacomini was not available for verification in depth. After he had contacted Dr. Liakhovsky and been left at liberty long enough to report to the German service his verification of Dolin's story, he disappeared. He was probably last seen with a group of "revolutionaries," friends of the man in the Okhta plant who had helped Dolin sabotage it.

The Germans now no longer doubted that Dolin was their man. His reputation as an extraordinarily successful German agent in Russia grew with each press report of sabotage; through him they controlled these teams of saboteurs inspired by revolutionary purposes. It was an important and costly enough operation that Colonel von Bismarck took charge of it personally, receiving and briefing Dolin on each of his visits from Russia to Bern. Up through February 1916 the military attaché kept giving him the bank drafts that duly found their way to Paris Okhrana.

Switch to Psywar

At one of their meetings, about the first of March 1916, Colonel von Bismarck sounded out Dolin about undertaking the promotion of German-directed psychological warfare in Russia. The various underground cells among factory workers and in urban neighborhoods which Dolin had described as his instruments for carrying out sabotage could perhaps now be even more useful in spreading defeatist propaganda. Dolin cautiously admitted there might be possibilities for mounting a far-flung campaign, at first strictly underground, then more open, with the major theme of ending the war with Germany and overthrowing Tzarism. Avoiding any untoward display of his own interest, he obliquely led Bismarck to see immense potential in

70   CONFIDENTIAL

4. *(Continued)*

a well-directed propaganda program. Bismarck then asked him whether he would undertake the job.

Dolin said he would have to study the offer. His whole career, he said, had been with the Russian underground's campaign of terror and sabotage; he had no experience in agitation and propaganda. The colonel would have to give him guidance. It would be helpful to know what psychological efforts had already been made and how effective they were judged to be. He was sure that all the underground cells he had contacts with would be anxious to cooperate, but they would have to be coordinated with any other existing assets and channels for pro-German propaganda in Russia. He would need a comprehensive view of the whole psywar plan.

During the rest of March and early April Bismarck personally undertook to prepare Dolin for his new job as director of the German propaganda program in Russia. In his briefings Dolin learned about a number of German operations hitherto unknown to the Russian services. Early in May he went to Russia to get the project going. As the dispatches reveal, he was again under constant Okhrana observation and given guidance and covert support for the purpose of convincing the Germans that he and his comrades in the underground cells were assiduously waging psychological warfare for them. This was another costly operation for the Germans, who regularly deposited funds in the Swiss banks to pay the purported warriors.

Came the Revolution

Dolin's case officer Colonel Erhardt had died in a Bordeaux hospital in May 1915, and his substitute case officer and partner in notional sabotage operations Litvin had been assigned to England to handle a group of agents engaged in wartime counterespionage. Station chief Krassilnikov had thus for some time now acted as Dolin's case officer. They frequently met, in various places in Paris, before and after the meetings with Bismarck. Their last encounter was in January 1917, when Dolin left for Russia on his final German assignment. He was about to lose his greatest gamble. The Okhrana files contain no further record of him.

Agafonov, in mentioning Dolin's suicide, does not say just when it occurred. It is known that the investigative commission sent by the provisional government to Paris in June 1917 made an intense search of the records of his double-agent role. Petrograd specifically requested this in February 1918 and was sent a report of the findings on

4. *(Continued)*

the eve of the Brest-Litovsk negotiations. It is conceivable that such a report could have been of use to the Bolshevik delegation discussing the armistice terms.

One striking aspect of this double-agent operation was the extreme confidence the Germans placed in Dolin. In the spring of 1915, when Dolin and Litvin were charged by Bismarck with deception, they took particular care to check whether they were being followed or investigated. They were never able to detect a thing. And so through 1915 and 1916, making his Okhrana contacts in Switzerland, Paris, or London, Dolin kept on guard but could find no hint of any effort to check up on him. The Germans apparently entertained no suspicion whatever after the Bismarck challenge and only learned at Brest Litovsk that their Dolin was not theirs.

The Okhrana stated its rationale for running Dolin as a double agent in the initial communications after the Germans offered to recruit him. The same reasoning was repeated in the dispatches reporting Bismarck's proposals for psychological warfare. The Germans, the argument went, would run or try to run sabotage operations and propaganda activities with or without Dolin. Consequently it would pay to let them engage Dolin and his notional underground cells, and do everything possible to convince them that he was performing efficiently. Happy with his success, they would put less effort into other such missions. The double operation would also give the Okhrana regular information on the enemy's intentions, methods, and program. It could at the same time help uncover any other German operations.

All these arguments were fully vindicated in the course of the operation, and Dolin's commendations from his chiefs at home and abroad were well deserved.

CONFIDENTIAL

Some anti-revolutionary operations of the imperial Russian political police.

THE OKHRANA'S FEMALE AGENTS [1]

Rita T. Kronenbitter

Part I: Russian Women

In a memorandum of 31 January 1911 addressed to the Police Department in Petersburg, the imperial MVD gave a description of Anna Gregoriyeva Serebryakova, the ideal of female agents:

"She had completed 25 years of continuous and very useful service for Moscow Okhrana. As a secret [penetration] agent she had connections with the leaders of many subversive organizations but was not attached anywhere as a regular or active member. Her motivation for hard agent work came from her strong personal convictions. She hated sedition in all forms and performed her assignments against subversives as an idealist, having little interest in monetary remuneration . . .

"She kept her secrets even from her family. Accepting the job of clandestine employment against the revolutionaries, she had to reconcile herself to exposing her own children to revolutionary propaganda by holding meetings of subversives in her home . . . Despite the emotional and spiritual conflicts she had to suppress unshared with anyone, her devotion to duty never failed."

The memorandum goes on to declare that Serebryakova, now ill, blind, and deserted by her family after Burtzev, chief of the revolutionaries' counterintelligence, exposed her in 1909 as an Okhrana agent, was to receive an annual pension of 1200 rubles in gratitude for her long and devoted service.

Personnel Practices

The Okhrana depended heavily on female agents, particularly in foreign operations, and Serebryakova came to be held up and fre-

---

[1] Most of the information in this article is derived from the collection *Zagranichnaya Okhrana* (The Okhrana Abroad) at the Hoover Institution, Stanford, California, consisting principally of the complete archives of the Okhrana station in Paris. For the story of operations within Russia, however, it has been necessary to use secondary sources—Agafonov, Vassiliyev, Zavarzin, and others.

CONFIDENTIAL

25

5.

quently pointed to as a model. The best of the female operatives, the records show, did have their paramount motivation in patriotism and devotion to the anti-revolutionary cause. But as in any intelligence service some were attracted by the danger and glamor of clandestine life, some were blackmailed into intelligence work, and many, especially those that were not Russian, had strictly mercenary motives. Later we shall trace some individual agent careers of all these kinds.

The records show that a number of Russian deep-cover agents were drawn into the service by some form of conversion after conviction as revolutionaries. Kovalskaya, "Gramm" (true name not recorded), Borovskaya, and Romanova are some of the ex-revolutionary women on the agent lists. After having served part of their terms in prisons or in exile, they were persuaded to work for the Okhrana, freed on some legal pretext, and normally helped to escape abroad to begin their agent activity. Although some of these converts in time became proficient and trusted employees, they were seldom accorded the same confidence as agents without prior leftist records.

Wives, mistresses, and sisters of male Okhrana agents were often a convenient source of recruits, particularly for operations abroad. When director Lopukhin sent Lev Beitner to Paris in 1905 with the assignment of collecting the intelligence required to control arms smuggling on the part of the revolutionaries, the agent took with him his wife and sister in order to engage in simultaneous operations in the capitals and ports of France, England, and the Low Countries. The three received their pay separately, but Beitner did the planning and gave the women their assignments. The operation was successful in uncovering every major shipment of arms in the Baltic and Black Seas.

"Julietta," Beitner's sister, in addition to her immense contribution in spotting clandestine arms sales, supply dumps, and cargo craft and crews, distinguished herself later by discovering and infiltrating the shop where Robert Loewenthal, an émigré from Russia, counterfeited Russian banknotes to finance the revolutionaries. She became Loewenthal's partner in the shop by giving 1000 francs, ostensibly from her savings but supplied by the Okhrana, for the purchase of some special printing equipment. She met daily with her case officer for the operation, an Okhrana staff agent, and they worked out a

26

5. *(Continued)*

detailed plan whereby the entire ring of producers and distributors could be taken red-handed.

Agent Brontman's mistress Eropkina played a similar role. Like Beitner, Brontman had served many successful years in Russia. When the Okhrana decided to send him abroad, it hired his mistress and sent her along with him. The two worked for a number of years as penetration agents, he in the Party of Socialist Revolutionaries, she with the Social Democrats (Bolsheviks).

It appears that the salaries of women agents were for the most part equal to those of men, and frequently they were even higher. Their code names and pseudonyms were usually male (while male agents were at times given female first names or nicknames—Katia. Lucy, Belle, and the like).

Okhrana staff officers were always men. Staff agents abroad, who did spotting, recruiting, and liaison work, controlled operations, and handled agents, were likewise always men. The archives of the Okhrana abroad have no record of a woman in the capacity of case officer. Women could be the most valuable of agents, engaged in extremely dangerous or sensitive operations, but they never held positions entailing any kind of supervisory function. The Okhrana offices at home likewise had no females on the staff except in clerical capacities; women served otherwise as agents only.

In this respect the Okhrana's practice contrasts sharply with that in revolutionary ranks. Lenin's wife Krupskaya, as the heavy Okhrana folders of her intercepted mail indicate, could be considered the de facto intelligence director for the Social Democratic Party (Bolshevik) and, in part, the Jewish Bundists. Much of her correspondence with fellow conspirators all over Europe and the Russian Empire was in secret writing; this was of many types and often complex. For years she was busy gathering information for the party and the revolution, sending out instructions, designing codes for communications, receiving and dispatching couriers, and acting as an informal but competent intelligence center.

The Okhrana's women were different from their counterparts among the revolutionaries in various other ways. They were predominantly Christian, i.e., Greek Orthodox when of Russian origin, while the revolutionary women, like most of the men, either were Jewish or belonged to some minority group of the Empire such as the Poles,

Armenians, or Latvians.[2] The only Jewish female agents sent abroad by the Okhrana seem to be those who accompanied their male partners to form operational teams like those of Beitner and Brontman mentioned above. But the Okhrana's male deep-cover agents abroad tended to be predominantly Jewish like the revolutionaries.

The files contain no record of any special training for the women sent abroad. All the outstanding ones, however, are shown to have spent some preparatory time in close association with the very top operators in Petersburg and Moscow. That time was presumably devoted to some kind of training, at least briefing on targets and methods of operation abroad. There is no indication of any other than strictly operational relationship between the bosses in Russia and the female agents. Abroad, the propaganda of the revolutionaries accused exposed female agents of being prostitutes or mistresses of their case officers, but the records give no reason to believe that the accusations were anything but convenient propaganda.

Some of the women agents were instructed to communicate directly, upon arrival in the field, with the chiefs at headquarters in Petersburg or at Moscow Okhrana; accommodation addresses were supplied at both ends. In all cases, however, it soon became the practice to channel communications through the field office in Paris or Berlin. The field offices then ultimately assigned case officers and exercised direct control over the agents.

Following are case histories of some of the individual Okhrana women, selected as typifying the operations and methods of the time. First come the stories of three Russian agents, then those of some indigenous recruits.[3]

Francesco

Dr. Nikolai Sergeyevich Zhuchenko, a physician of excellent professional reputation and high standing in the Moscow society of 1913, made a discreet inquiry at the police department concerning the whereabouts of his wife Zinaida. She had left him full fifteen years ago

---

[3] Paris Okhrana files contain about 75,000 cards on some 20,000 Russian exiles abroad. These operational records cover known and suspected revolutionaries, members of Anarchist, terrorist, Socialist, and similar groups. The names and personal descriptions reveal that over 75 percent of them were Jewish and about 10 percent were from other minority groups, leaving less than 15 percent Russian. The card file of Okhrana secret operatives abroad shows an even greater proportion of Jewish agents.

[3] These latter in Part II, to appear in a future issue.

84

5. *(Continued)*

to go into hiding from the police, and she had not been heard from again. The doctor, being a good and law-abiding citizen, had never approved of her revolutionary associations during their five years of married life together, and for that reason her disappearance had not unduly upset him. Now he had decided that fifteen years was long enough to wait; he wanted to know whether she was dead or alive. In fact, he wanted to remarry.

As was usual with such inquiries, this found its way to the Okhrana identity section in Moscow. Zinaida's name was there, but the card contained only a reference to another set of identity records kept at Okhrana headquarters. In Petersburg Zinaida's card and voluminous operational dossier were located under the name "Francesco."

Matters under this operational code name were of utmost importance and sensitive enough to require the personal attention of the chief. Police Director Aleksei Vassiliyev wrote to Paris, instructing Paris Okhrana chief Krassilnikov to have a talk with agent Francesco, Mme. Zhuchenko. The Okhrana chiefs were just as anxious as the parties concerned to avoid a divorce suit in the open courts. The lady turned out to be agreeable to a quiet divorce. She asked that the doctor be told she was no longer in hiding but in Paris and still active as a revolutionary. He should be given her Paris address in order to simplify negotiation on the divorce.[1]

Paris Okhrana files contain many references to Francesco, but the bulk of her operational dossier was probably removed to Petersburg after she was exposed by revolutionary intelligence and denounced as an Okhrana agent. It is possible also that a revolutionary commission which came to Paris in 1917 to search the Okhrana records removed some of the papers on her. This account of her career is therefore sketchy and drawn in part from general histories of the Okhrana. All early writers about the service devote considerable space to her position among the revolutionaries and her accomplishments against them.

Apprenticeship

Zinaida, daughter of a government official named Guerngross and graduate of the Smolny Institute in Petersburg, was still a student at Moscow University when she made three vows, all at about the same time. She took the marriage vow with young Doctor Zhuchenko;

---

[1] Paris Okhrana files, Incoming Dispatches, 1913, No. 1465.

CONFIDENTIAL   29

5. *(Continued)*

she took oath with a group of university students conspiring to kill the Czar; and she swore to serve faithfully as an Okhrana agent. From the beginning, her career shows that she took only the last of these seriously. Even during her five years of married life she could not settle down to relatively prosperous ease as a housewife; to her husband's distress she associated with revolutionaries and malcontents of all brands.

Her refusal to single out any one subversive group and become a member may have been due to her husband's protest, but it was more likely in conformity with the Okhrana's doctrine that the most dependable agent is one who succeeds in developing access to all revolutionary groups without belonging to any.[2] In her later operations, as she forged the reputation of being one of the two most important of all Okhrana agents at home and abroad,[3] she adhered strictly to this doctrine. The other of the two, Evno Azev, contrastingly, forever strove to attain top positions among the revolutionaries, frequently by means of betraying his rivals to the Okhrana.

Zinaida, according to a case officer's description of her as a student at the fashionable Smolny Institute, was thoroughly opposed to revolutionary activities but had a love for adventure and challenging risks. Even at this time, before her recruitment, she expressed her conviction that the revolutionaries had a corrupting and demoralizing effect upon students and the people in general. An eager recruit, she followed instructions with enthusiasm and was perspicacious and adventurous enough to penetrate subversive groups and bands of conspirators beyond her assigned targets. Her case officers[4] first required reports on individuals, groups, activities, and plans. Much of her year or so under her Moscow case officer, Zubatov, must have been devoted to training and some to a cooling-off period. But by 1895 she had already attained the distinction, though probably known then only to Zubatov, of having saved the life of Czar Nicolas II.

In the spring of that year Moscow students worked out a plan to kill the Czar. One of them was assigned to throw a bomb from a steeple of the Church of Ivan the Terrible down on the imperial

---

[2] Pavel P. Zavarzine, *Souvenirs d'un Chef de l'Okhrana*, p. 21.

[3] Boris Nikolaevsky, *Aseff: the Russian Judas*, p. 158.

[4] Her case officer in Petersburg in 1893 was Colonel Semyakin, who introduced her in 1894 to the chief organizer of the Okhrana's penetration service, Zubatov. The latter, as chief of operations in Moscow, remained her case officer until her removal in 1895.

30   CONFIDENTIAL

5. *(Continued)*

cortege as it passed below. The chemists in the conspiracy fashioned the device and it was delivered to a nearby monastery. Zinaida waited until the preparations were finished and the conspirators were all in place, and then gave the word. All were arrested, including Zinaida, and deported to Siberia. There it was arranged that she, along with several others as a screen, could make good an escape.

Trial by Terror

Zinaida thus went abroad as an escaped Siberian exile and began operations under Arkadi Harting, chief of the Okhrana's Berlin outpost, who assigned her tasks in Berlin and Leipzig. She was soon called to other European countries, but her principal target became the Socialist Revolutionaries and their Fighting Unit (*Boyevaya druzhina*) which carried out assassinations and other kinds of terror in Russia.

Paralleling Zubatov in Moscow, Harting was the counter-intelligence planner *par excellence* abroad. His successes as a provocation agent in Paris in 1890 had launched him on an intelligence career that took him to the very top of the Okhrana ladder. In Berlin he relied heavily upon Zinaida's work, not only as her case officer but as chief of operations in Germany. The two worked together as the most successful team of the period. When Harting left Berlin to take charge of the integrated Okhrana station in Paris, Francesco, to use her code name, remained in Heidelberg with instructions to concentrate on the Socialist Revolutionaries through active participation in their Fighting Unit for purposes of control.

Active participation soon meant trouble for Francesco. The revolutionaries had reason to suspect treachery in their ranks: too many conspirators sent to Russia to commit atrocities were being apprehended. Francesco was among those who had knowledge of all of these, and the central committee of the party may have had other grounds for suspecting her in particular. Now the customary means of testing the loyalty of a member under suspicion was to assign acts of terror to him. Francesco was accordingly, in 1905, made leader of one of three assassination teams to be dispatched simultaneously to Russia. She personally was to carry out her team's assignment, the assassination of General Kurlov, governor of Minsk.

This assignment posed a veritable dilemma before the Okhrana. If it wanted Francesco to remain in the Fighting Unit and continue her good work, she would have to carry out the assassination. A

5. *(Continued)*

solution was worked out by Colonel Klimovich of Moscow Okhrana. Francesco consented to carry out the assassination as instructed. She met with her team of assistants and planned the details of the action—how, when, and where she would throw the bomb. But from her lodgings she took the bomb to an Okhrana safe house, where an expert disarmed the detonator and made it a dud. When it was thrown at General Kurlov nothing happened.

In the meantime the other two teams had been successful in their assassinations. Mme. Zhuchenko, Francesco, had given ample warnings of them, but there had been a slip-up somewhere in Colonel Klimovich's plans to prevent them. In the course of investigating these acts of terror, Kurlov turned up the name Zhuchenko, and his pursuit of this lead was eventually to cause the exposure of her agent work. Not knowing that she had actually saved his life, the governor made so much fuss about her that her true status had to be made known to certain Okhrana personnel that did not otherwise need to know. Among these was a Leonid Menshchikov, who in 1910 defected to the revolutionary intelligence service and betrayed her.

Successful and Sought After

Before that eventuality, however, Francesco had five more years of continuous, prolific service. Now the conspirators fully trusted her, after she had personally participated in the triple assassination, two-thirds successful; they could not hold her responsible that her bomb turned out to be a dud. Terrorist groups were liquidated by the authorities one after another, thanks in considerable measure to her reports and forewarnings. Large-scale bank and other robberies, euphemistically called "expropriations" by the revolutionaries, failed after her alert.

These extraordinary achievements gained Francesco a name as Okhrana's ace agent at home and abroad. The top leaders at headquarters, in Moscow, and in Paris, the only ones supposed to know her identity, vied for her services. A set of cables and letters in a folder labeled Mikheyev—this was her pseudonym for interoffice correspondence—shows a tug-of-war for her between Harting in Paris and Colonel Klimovich in Moscow. Klimovich's demands for her transfer finally ceased after Harting sent the following cable. (The French words were carried in clear text among the encoded Russian, here translated to English.)

5. *(Continued)*

"*Veuillez* stop asking for Mikheyev. *Semblables procédés impossibles*. I shall never approve transfer . . . I consider such attitudes among colleagues in the same service unpardonable . . . Stealing agents from each other only makes more difficulties for our intelligence efforts . . ."

By 1906 Mme. Zhuchenko's monthly pay had been raised to 500 rubles, ample to let her move about as a fairly well-to-do lady. In addition there were liberal presents for Christmas and Easter, bonuses for major exposures of assassination and burglary projects, and allowances for travel and other operational expense. She had a son, her only personal responsibility, whom she kept in Berlin even when on prolonged assignments in Moscow. Her home was in Berlin's western suburb of Charlottenburg.

The End

That is where she was when exposed by the defector Menshchikov. Burtzev, chief of counterintelligence for the revolutionaries, solemnly called on her. He explained in his methodical and unexcited way that his intelligence penetration of the Okhrana made it completely clear to him that she was an Okhrana agent, that the central committee had already sentenced her to death, and that he would personally guarantee her life if she would come clean, confess, and thenceforth help him in the fight against the Okhrana. She refused, and reported promptly to her case officer, Colonel von Kotten.

Soon all the revolutionary press published her name as one of the most vicious agents-provocateurs ever exposed. The Berlin police provided the necessary protection for her, but she had to be pensioned off—at pay higher than her active wages had been. Resigned to her retirement, she said to Von Kotten, "In this profession no one can be safe from traitors and betrayals. The fall of my life has come after rich and active labors in the spring and summer." But Zavarzin, Vassiliyev, and other authors have written that she still continued to make useful reports on the revolutionaries. None of them knew what finally became of her.

In 1910 she was about 45 years old but looked younger. Zavarzin described her then as a tall, slender blonde, wearing glasses with round gold frames on a small nose under her large forehead, in short not particularly attractive and far from beautiful. But her speech, he said, was most pleasant, firm, and precise, usually serious and giving an impression of extraordinary character and intelligence.

5. *(Continued)*

Reminiscing about the long line of conspiracies broken up by her reporting, her eyes were animated as she described subterfuges she had used to escape from difficult situations.

She knew that reforms were needed in Russia but was convinced that a better life could not be achieved through the Communists' proletarian revolution or the Socialist Revolutionaries' terror and agrarian revolt. For herself she had only one real aim in life, to bring up her son properly. Music was her main recreation, and she attended the opera frequently. Knowing society well and feeling at home among all classes of people, from monarchists and aristocrats to underground subversives of all colors and morals, she was well equipped for her dedicated work.

Ulyanova

The Okhrana had recruited Roman Vatslavovich Malinovski, a Communist and personal friend of Lenin, in March 1910. Within a few months it selected him for all-out clandestine support as candidate for the Imperial Duma. He was active in the Metal Workers Union and a good orator. Some behind-the-scenes campaigning, the obedient good will of the gendarmes, and a supply of money from the Okhrana overcame all handicaps, even his prohibitive court record of having been jailed for common thievery. The Okhrana just had to have a penetration among the dozen or so Socialist and Communist deputies. That little fraction was numerically insignificant in the unwieldy Duma, but it was the only body of deputies who knew what they wanted and how to plan their action. And Okhrana agent "Ulyanova," who had been reporting on them profusely and religiously, had been terminated on 14 June.

Letter from a Lady

Ulyanova's true name was Julia Orestova Serova. In signing her reports she used another alias—Pravdivy, Truthful. She was an educated and rather literary woman, a member of the Social Democratic Workers Party (Bolshevik) who had never taken a very active part in its affairs. She had probably joined it to please her husband, who was a militant Bolshevik, committee member, archivist of the party, and its first deputy in the Duma.

The Okhrana's record of Ulyanova's life and work is replete with contradictions. She was described as a weak character, yet her steady and painstaking contributions to the service reveal a hard and con-

34

5. *(Continued)*

scientious worker. She loved her husband and was a faithful wife, but she betrayed him daily with reports on his political activities. She was described as frugal and a good housewife, yet it was need for money that recruited her and she was hungry for bonuses and awards on top of her regular monthly pay. Among the party affiliates she was spoken of as a saint and a quiet devotee, she who probably had no equal in betraying their trust and causing their arrest in groups.

She first made contact with the Okhrana in 1905, a write-in. In a letter dated 1 March she offered, for 1000 rubles, to give the underground locations where the committee of the Social Democratic Workers Party could be found. She was invited to come to the Fontanka, Okhrana headquarters in Petersburg, under secure arrangements. She did not obtain 1000 rubles, but half that sum was also considerable in the days when an average bourgeois family could live on it for six months. Soon thereafter the entire committee of the party was under arrest.

Ulyanova appears not to have expected this single betrayal to lead to any regular connections with the Okhrana. She needed the money at the moment but was not interested in continued employment thereafter. But Okhrana headquarters, quite pleased with the first transaction, was inclined otherwise. A case officer saw her. He knew about the clerical work she did for the party; how simple it would be for her to bring him information from the underground office. By collaborating she would be freed of fear of being watched herself. No one would suspect her. And it would give her a regular income. She refused.

But the case officer had her signature on a receipt for 500 rubles. Resorting to simple blackmail, he pointed out that what she had already done might easily become known, and she would lose her husband and family. Or she might land in the Fortress of Peter and Paul where those whom she had betrayed were prisoners, and they might find out that the new prisoner was the one who had reported on them. Faced with these consequences of refusal, Ulyanova agreed to continue. She submitted irregular reports until September 1907, when, having by now become a willing and even enthusiastic agent, she signed a regular contract providing compensation at 25 rubles a month, which eventually grew to 150 a month.

In the Spirit of Service

Although her assignment required her to report only on the Petersburg Bolsheviks' internal affairs, she soon extended her purview to several other subversive groups. Her husband had many connections. Serov felt completely safe in his own home. He had a good, taciturn wife with political views identical to his own, and it would not have occurred to him not to introduce her to visiting fellow conspirators.

Numerous arrests were made in Petersburg and other cities as a result of Ulyanova's disclosures. In May 1907 her reports made possible the capture of an entire revolutionary band which, operating out of Vilna, was about to perform a set of "expropriations" from banks and the state treasury. In the same city they led to the discovery of a load of forbidden literature, including brochures and leaflets calling for an armed uprising. For this she got a 300-ruble special award. In September her information provided legal grounds for the arrest of Sergei Saltykov, a Duma deputy. Her reward of 500 rubles for this was paid on the day she signed on as a regular contract agent.

Through 1908 Ulyanova kept the Okhrana informed on all meetings of the Bolshevik central committee, the composition and structure of the organization, and the personnel of many local committees. In April of that year her information led to the arrest of four militants, among them Trotzky's brother-in-law Kamenev, in May to the capture of an entire underground gathering, and in September to the apprehension of Dubrovski, another member of the central committee. In February 1909 she brought about the exposure and liquidation of a revolutionary printshop in Petersburg and one for counterfeiting passports. Later that year the Bolsheviks sent her abroad to attend a conference, and in this connection she made a report on Aleksei Rykov.

These are just the recorded highlights of Ulyanova's work of disruption among the Bolsheviks. Her sources were always authentic, derived from her attendance at underground meetings, where she frequently served as recorder and general administrative assistant, and from activities in her own home, where her husband handled party matters and received fellow conspirators. She was an avid correspondent, and among the many letters she wrote to friends there were interspersed, sometimes daily, reports for delivery to the Okhrana.

Her sizable salary and awards would probably have led her to disaster sooner or later, for she began to spend far beyond her legitimate means. Some gossip about this had reached her husband, but

5. *(Continued)*

he remained trustful and never doubted her explanation that she got money from her family, who were not poor. Her undoing came from her own carelessness. As her zeal and practice in the work increased, she became slack in her precautions, often copying from her husband's papers right at his desk. One spring day in 1910, coming home unexpectedly, he caught her copying his confidential record of a meeting held with his Bolshevik deputy colleagues the preceding night.

Outcast

Serova tried to make a confused explanation, but he grabbed all the papers and saw that she had done the copying in the form of a letter to a friend. "Who is the friend?" Persistently evasive answers to his questions brought him to the point of violence. After giving her a thorough beating on the spot, he chased her out of the house, forbidding her ever to return. She took their two small children with her, and she never did return. On 10 June Serov ran a notice in the Petersburg newspaper to the effect that he no longer considered Julia Orestova his wife.

Okhrana director Beletzky fully understood what this announcement meant. Four days after it was published a memorandum was added to Ulyanova's dossier recording that her name had been deleted from the roster of secret agents. A copy of this memorandum came to the attention of the Minister of Interior, who was acquainted with Ulyanova's record. He demanded an explanation from Beletzky. Why should such an extraordinarily productive and frequently rewarded agent be subject to sudden termination? The explanation, of course, was convincing.

From then on hounded by her husband, without friends, and without income, Ulyanova from time to time contacted her Okhrana bosses. In August 1912 she pleaded urgently for help: "My two children, one only five years old, are without clothes, and we have no food. I have sold everything, even furniture; I have no work, and if you do not help me I will end as a suicide." She was given 150 rubles. Other letters followed, sometimes pressing and desperate, not seldom threatening suicide. All of them elicited some amount or other, 50, 100, 200 rubles, until they totaled 1800 rubles at the end of 1912. One last letter after that brought her 300 rubles and an order to leave Petersburg for good. She was given transportation for herself and children to any place she wanted to go.

CONFIDENTIAL   37

5. *(Continued)*

Serova found another husband during the war. Just before the first revolution of 1917, she addressed a final letter to headquarters in Petersburg:

"I would like you to recall my good and loyal services. On the eve of great events that we all feel are coming, it hurts me to stay inactive and unable to be useful. My second husband is an excellent man and worthy of your confidence. It would not be difficult for me to have him join the Bolsheviks and guide him in the procurement of intelligence. You must realize that that party has to be watched very closely now in the interest of all——our Czar, our Empire, and our armies."

The letter was never answered. She and her husband both perished in the revolution.

Sharzh, Sharni, Sharli, Charlie, Shalnoi

The Okhrana used these code names for Mme. Zagorskaya, who had a remarkably long record of continuous service as an agent and was the highest paid of them all. Her targets were the top leaders among the Socialist Revolutionaries, the terrorists, and the Anarchists. She worked under the direct supervision of three successive chiefs of Paris Okhrana, beginning with Ratayev in 1903, then Harting, and finally Krassilnikov until February 1917.

Because she was handled by the chief rather than staff agents who would have to report in detail to the chief, Paris Okhrana files are rather meager concerning her activities and stages of growth as an agent. Her full name was Maria Alekseyevna Zagorskaya, *née* Andreyevna. She was married to Peter Frantsevich Zagorski, another Okhrana agent, who was a Catholic and originally came from Croatia in the Austro-Hungarian Empire. At times the couple worked as a team, but she scored her major achievements in her singleton operations.

Socialite Couple

Zagorski had begun his agent work in 1901, having been hired by the Okhrana's staff agent Manusevich-Manuilov in Rome and given the task of reporting on Polish and Catholic émigrés from Russia. His wife-to-be was recruited not long after by Ratayev, as head of the Okhrana personnel section in Petersburg just before his departure to become chief of the Paris station. The two new agents met at

38

5. *(Continued)*

Petersburg when Manuilov brought the young Croat to headquarters for training.

The Okhrana files contain no record of the married life of the couple. They were assigned abroad in early 1903 to work with Ratayev, but there the record of Zagorski himself stops for several years. He is described as unusually well qualified, having encyclopedic knowledge of geography, economics, arts, people, etc. He was therefore not used for ordinary anti-revolutionary operations but frequently assigned to missions involving travel as an Austrian subject, on which he would report directly to the police directorate. At one time he associated with Pilsudski and other Polish and Russian rebels and top Anarchists.

Later Zagorski changed his Austrian citizenship to French, and the couple established a home in Paris. When the revolutionaries, after Azev's exposure, started a vigorous campaign to uncover all the Okhrana's penetrations, the Zagorskis came under considerable suspicion. Both of them were apparently without employment of any kind, yet they lived in lordly luxury and gave sumptuous parties. Zagorskaya, however, casually let slip food for gossip about their family wealth, and her parents were soon spoken of as rich merchants while he became known as a great landowner in Croatia. This tactic was successful and suspicion subsided, especially since it was widely understood that they distributed a good deal of their wealth in donations to various subversive causes.

Zagorskaya's chief task in all her fifteen years of service was to penetrate the leading groups of the Party of Socialist Revolutionaries and its Fighting Unit at home and abroad. To this end she had joined the party in Petersburg and won the confidence of the underground as a capable member who could do much for the cause abroad. She had no difficulty making herself useful not only in the central committee of the party headquarters in Paris but among the leaders of the terrorist Fighting Unit. For years she was a close friend and associate of the mistress of Boris Savinkov, leader of the Fighting Unit, and she maintained a steady correspondence with Russian terrorists in France, Italy, and England.

Belittled by New Boss

Her pay was high enough to let her live in grand style. Her income from her agent work was 3500 French francs a month, about that

5. *(Continued)*

of cabinet ministers of the period. It was higher than Krassilnikov's salary when he became chief of Paris Okhrana in 1910. He did not particularly relish this situation, and he wrote headquarters that her accomplishments were not worth the amounts paid her in salary and operational expenses. He not only wanted her salary lowered but recommended that he stop handling her directly and turn her over to his principal staff agent, Lt. Col. Erhardt.

It was generally agreed that her services were now less valuable than under Ratayev and Harting, from 1903 to 1909, and so her salary and expense allowance was cut to 2500 francs a month. But Krassilnikov did not succeed in transferring her to the staff agent. She enjoyed considerable protection at headquarters, and Okhrana director Vissarionov himself saw to it that her wishes about who should direct her work were honored.

But Krassilnikov persisted. In 1912 he decided to transfer Zagorskaya to staff agent Erhardt regardless of what attitude headquarters might take about it. Then she wrote, in her own typescript, directly to Vissarionov:

> Esteemed Sergei Evlampiyevich:
> A. A. [Aleksandr Aleksandrovich Krassilnikov] told me he received orders to discontinue contact with me and transfer me to a different person. He has been proposing this transfer for some time, but I have always refused to be transferred and I still insist on refusing. The reasons A. A. gives for this transfer are not valid, and the transfer would cause an unnecessary change in my life. A. A. is known by name and address to many as an official representative, but he maintains no open contact with the person to whom he wants to assign me. I find that dealing with this new man would be inconvenient and even dangerous. (I do not need to go into particulars, you can see for yourself why it would be dangerous for me.) Dealing with A. A. directly would assure me that our contact will remain strictly clandestine and dependable. A. A. is well known and I can maintain contact with him, like so many others, without fear for my security.
> Please consider this aspect—the psychological effect of transferring an agent from one case officer to another. One does not have to be subtle to comprehend the feelings of an agent transferred to a new case officer. You recall our work together, and you can understand that my work is bound to suffer severely from the change . . .

The lengthy letter begged that Krassilnikov be ordered to continue handling her. Headquarters, after some vacillation, complied, and there was no change in case officer.

5. *(Continued)*

To the End

Zagorskaya remained in Okhrana employ until the revolution of February 1917. Her husband, however, after joining the French army in 1914, was released to fight with the Yugoslav volunteer army on the Salonica front. Agafonov, writing about the Okhrana and its agents from the revolutionary point of view, claims that Zagorski was exposed as an Austrian agent by the Serbs at Salonica. Considering, however, that it was normal Serbian practice to hang all suspects, one may suppose that this allegation was only added coloring to paint the agent still more despicable in the eyes of the Russian revolutionaries.

After the war the Zagorski couple lived quietly in retirement on the French Riviera.

CONFIDENTIAL

*Some foreign operations of the
Tzar's political police.*

THE OKHRANA'S FEMALE AGENTS

PART II: Indigenous Recruits [1]

Rita T. Kronenbitter

From the early stages of its existence the Okhrana adhered to a firm policy of strictly segregating its truly clandestine services. It divided agents into two categories, "external" and "internal," meaning roughly overt and covert respectively. The external agents were investigators. They did open and clandestine surveillance and a variety of detective work, including cooperation with other government security agencies at home and abroad. Whether known to the public as Okhrana employees or not, they were officially recognized within the government and paid overtly by it. The internal service, in contrast, was essentially a system of penetrations and thus by necessity completely secret. Its personnel were unknown not only to the public and other government agencies but for the most part to Okhrana officers themselves. The identity of its agents was masked even in the operational files recording their activities. Each was known personally only to his case officer and, usually, the chief of the unit he worked for; agents did not know of one another's existence.

Similarly no external agent was ever supposed to know an internal one, who would normally be operating under some revolutionary cover. So strictly was this rule enforced that an external agent who learned the identity of an internal agent would be dismissed. Thus it often happened that it was the duty of an external agent to mount surveillance on an internal agent ostensibly working for a subversive group. One obvious advantage of this circumstance was to provide a multiple check on the veracity and dependability of the penetration

---

[1] For Part I, *Russian Women*, see *Studies* IX 2, p. 25 ff. These articles are based primarily on the Hoover Institution's collection *Zagranichnaya Okhrana*, consisting chiefly of the Okhrana files from Paris, the main center of Russian revolutionary and anti-revolutionary activity abroad before World War I. These files, presented after the revolution to Herbert Hoover by the Kerenski government, have only recently been opened to the public.

CONFIDENTIAL

59

agents, a number of whom turned out to be playing a double role; but this was just a side benefit from the compartmentation practiced for the sake of the internal agents' security.

The principle of two separate categories of agents lent itself remarkably well to the operating problems of the Okhrana stations abroad. The first chief in Paris, Pëtr Ivanovich Rachkovsky (he held the post from 1884 to 1902), soon realized that external agents of Russian nationality were totally unsuitable for work in western Europe. Not just their language but their very appearance and behavior gave them away immediately. Gradually, therefore, all the Russian investigators were returned home and replaced by French, Italian, German, and British agents. The Okhrana abroad thus reinforced the functional dichotomy of the two agent categories with an ethnic one: foreigners, recruited largely from among host government and private detectives, became the investigators, while agents from Russia were devoted to penetration operations against the revolutionaries.

In the fall of 1913, however, most of Paris Okhrana's external, investigation agents were exposed by the revolutionaries' counterintelligence. In the ensuing upheaval former investigator Jollivet was suddenly transformed into a penetration agent inside the revolutionary service. Paris Okhrana found it expedient also to be flexible in the use of an array of mistresses of Monsieur Henri Bint.

The Women of Henri Bint

This Alsatian gentleman, hired by Rachkovsky in 1885 after ten years of service with the French *Sûreté*, remained one of the Paris station's principal investigators until the first world war. (During the war the Okhrana took him off routine investigation work and supplied him with funds to establish a residence in Switzerland, from where he could get agents into Germany and Austria. The Swiss imprisoned him in January 1917.) Apparently he never married, but he was never without mistresses, one at a time after he had learned quite early that it was neither healthy nor economical to have two or more together.

Life on the Riviera

Another thing Bint learned was to avail himself of the help his mistresses could render in connection with his job. In 1912, as leader of a surveillance network on the Riviera, he took along a mistress and loaned her free of charge both to a younger agent of his network

60   CONFIDENTIAL

6. *(Continued)*

named Fontana and to officers of the French and Italian police departments cooperating with him. This generosity led on one occasion to a serious contretemps. The mistress, staying with Fontana at a hotel in La Spezia, stole from his suitcase a batch of photographs and letters and gave them to a cooperating Italian agent, and there ensued a fist fight in one of the city's public squares. The police interfered, the press got interested, and there were provocative stories in French and Italian newspapers. Bint, although it was not entirely his fault, received a stern reprimand from the chief.

Bint had been dismissed from the Okhrana on two occasions, primarily on account of indecorous relations with the fair sex, but both times he was promptly rehired. The chiefs valued his professional skill and realized that he occasionally got results from his mistresses' peeping into the activities of unreliable Russian aristocrats in Paris. Although a French demoiselle could not understand what the Russians were saying among themselves, she could keep company with individual conspirators, who could all speak some French. By using his girls Bint thus became more than a mere detective; the information they procured was almost in the category of that from internal agents.

Understandably enough, however, the system gradually wore out: the revolutionaries became wary of Parisian female companions. Then in 1911, when Bint's colleague Leroi defected from the Okhrana to join Burtzev's revolutionary counterintelligence, Bint had to cut off all *espiéglerie* with the females, as the practice was called. Bint and Leroi had worked together for years against the same targets, using the same techniques and often sharing mistresses for whatever job was on hand. No one cursed Leroi so much as Bint for his defection; he knew he would tell Burtzev all about it. He even anticipated that on Leroi's advice Burtzev would sooner or later try the trick on him, hiring some female to work on him. And so he did.

Tables Turned

Liubov Julia was a Parisian whose first name suggested Russian origin. The use of Julia as a surname was most likely her own invention. When Bint first saw her, in a public café, she was with a group of revolutionaries, but she seemed much too frivolous and gay to be concerned with politics or conspiracies. She acted like any ordinary Parisian *demimondaine* of the period. He made her acquaintance and found that she was just as jolly in his company as she had seemed among the Russian intellectuals. At the moment

6. *(Continued)*

he was not particularly tied to any mistress, so he took her home with him, and there she stayed.

This was early 1913. He reported in full to his Okhrana superiors. His case officer thought that Julia might prove useful in work among the revolutionaries, cables and dispatches were exchanged with Petersburg headquarters, and Julia was hired under the code name "Jourdain." She was to receive 100 francs a month for reporting to Bint on several groups of conspirators in Paris.

Thus there happened to Bint what he was afraid would happen: he had a mistress spy on him just as he had used mistresses to spy on others. Julia was Burtzev's plant. She would regularly bring Bint quantities of attractive information, all written in her own hand, which always turned out to be of little or no value to the Okhrana. Bint's case officer, who had reports about Julia's activities from other sources, soon decided that she ought to be able to produce much better intelligence. Gradually it was possible to check the sources of the information she delivered, and it was discovered that all of it was prepared by Burtzev's counterintelligence people.

Just about this time Julia suddenly came forth with a demand for 500 francs in cash, threatening to sue Bint and expose him in the French press. She was dismissed at once. In the lengthy explanations dispatched to headquarters toward the end of 1913, the Paris station maintained that Julia could not possibly have gained access to any information about the Okhrana and could not even have supplied Burtzev with any knowledge about Bint except the fact of his physical association with her.

A Woman Scorned

Burtzev and Leroi had had even less success in an earlier, somewhat dissimilar attempt. In 1908 Henri Bint made the acquaintance of Lea Chauvin, and she stayed in his apartment, on and off, collaborating in his professional work, for some three years until in 1911, shortly after Leroi's defection, Bint was called to Petersburg. It was not customary to bring non-Russian external agents to headquarters, but he, as the most important sleuth of three decades and chief manager of the network of detectives, was made an exception. The consultation with him was to include some training, which would entail his absence from Paris for many weeks, possibly two or three months.

By age, Bint could have been Lea's grandfather. Although he always preferred young girls, this affair had lasted much longer than

62

6. *(Continued)*

usual and his leaving for Petersburg seemed a good occasion to close it off. He told the girl that it would be sensible for her to find someone more suitable to her age. But she did not want to be sensible. She refused to leave; she would stay in the apartment and wait for his return. Bint would not have it. There were several rough scenes, and when she still refused to go he had to call the police to make her get out.

Lea was in a fighting, vengeful mood. She would never have obeyed Bint's order to leave; the ingrate had to call the police to throw her out. That was what she told Leroi, who somehow learned of her distress and promptly called on her to offer consolation. Leroi of course knew all about Lea's life with Bint. He himself had always had a soft spot for her, but now she might have information about Bint's recent activities and the purpose of his trip to Petersburg. In this emotional state she even seemed a good prospect for agent work—well motivated and familiar with Bint's contacts and operations.

After much talk about his friendship and understanding for her feelings, Leroi persuaded Lea to visit Burtzev's office. She was ready for anything as long as it meant hurting Bint, and Burtzev and Leroi found it easy to recruit her for intelligence work against Bint and against the Okhrana that had taken him away from her. Leroi's enthusiasm for the prospective operation was probably enhanced by his fondness for Lea, but Burtzev trusted his judgment. He had made him chief investigator in all operations against the Okhrana's non-Russian networks.

For a short time Lea became as much devoted to Leroi as she had been to Bint, but soon she seemed to have developed some second thoughts. Who can tell what was really in her mind? Maybe she thought she could reawaken the affections of her dear old Bint when he returned, or perhaps she developed an aversion to the rather uncouth and frequently drunk Leroi. Whatever the reason, after everything was agreed and she was to become an agent of the revolutionary counterintelligence, she secretly went to see the chief of Paris Okhrana, Aleksandr Aleksandrovich Krassilnikov. Yet this was just a probing action; all she did was complain about how Bint had thrown her out on the street. In relaying her story to headquarters, Krassilnikov wrote that he had given her 500 francs to keep her quiet and recover from her a packet of Bint's personal letters which she had appropriated to use just in case.

6. *(Continued)*

Lea was astonished by the 500 francs. She had never had that much money in her hand before. She became bemused with the possibilities of earning more; she had already observed that the revolutionary intelligence office was short of funds. So she made a second visit to Krassilnikov, and this time she told him all about how Burtzev and Leroi had recruited her to work for them and assured her of a steady income. She said she did not trust Leroi, he had deserted his friend Bint, and he would desert her the same way. Finally she offered her services to Krassilnikov, saying that she knew from living with Bint and helping him just what she would have to do to be useful.

Redoubled Hero

A case officer was assigned, and soon thereafter Lea's reports were being dispatched to headquarters under the code name "L'héros." The Okhrana instructed her to stay on the job in Burtzev's office and report on every assignment she received. At first it was just debriefings: one lengthy report on a luncheon with Burtzev and Leroi told of pressing questions on the current whereabouts of Harting, former Paris Okhrana chief, and hundreds of questions on the orders received by Bint, the times and places he would meet with Okhrana officers, his non-Russian affiliates, and his methods for receiving pay and instructions and submitting reports. As a double agent working in Burtzev's office with the position of assistant to Leroi, she was paid 200 francs a month by the Okhrana.

Mme. Chauvin, as she was introduced to visiting revolutionaries in Burtzev's office, delighted her chiefs there by her willingness to be of use, though she was disappointingly ill acquainted with the operational information they wanted. Burtzev decided to use her in other operations. Once Leroi took her to Place Bouveau, in front of the Ministry of the Interior and the *Sûreté Générale*, gave her a camera, and told her to take pictures of a man he would point out leaving the building. This project of Leroi's was soon brought to the attention of the Okhrana liaison officer in the *Sûreté*, M. Moreau, chief of the political police who, it happened, was the man whose picture Leroi wanted.

Another time Leroi took her to a lawyer named Tomasini, who she found out later was a naturalized Frenchman of Russian origin. The two wanted a statement from her to the effect that Bint had been receiving from the Monyjeux District post office a number of letters

6. *(Continued)*

addressed to Russian revolutionaries. (Burtzev repeatedly tried to prove that Paris postal officials were selling revolutionary correspondence to the Okhrana.) Lea replied that she knew nothing of any such mail being given to Bint. They pleaded with her for a long time to write and sign such a deposition. Though they offered her 1,000 francs cash and the assurance of 200 francs a month for the rest of her life, according to her report forwarded in a dispatch to Petersburg, she answered only that she could not affirm what she did not know.

Dispatches to Petersburg in the Paris Okhrana files show that L'héros continued as a double agent until the outbreak of the war. Her pay was increased to 275 francs a month, delivered to her regularly by Bint, who on his return became her case officer, nothing more this time.

Jane

Marcel Bittard-Monin, supervisor of most of Paris Okhrana's non-Russian agents, made Mme. G. Richard Le Davadie sign five papers relating to the termination of her service. She was furious. The smooth talk with which the goaty Lothario tried to cheer her in her misery only enraged her more; he was taking the side of the Russian bosses. She didn't give a damn, she said, what new twists they were taking in their policy. She could not care less whether they conformed to the attitude of the French government. What she wanted and needed was the job they were taking away.

She felt cheated by this sudden deprivation not only of income but of everything she had enjoyed for a half dozen interesting years of spying—first for Bittard personally and then for the Okhrana behind him. She had had tours at the best times of year to the Côte d'Azur and the Italian Riviera, all expenses paid. In the endless variety of tasks that she performed she had earned much praise, which always made her feel happy, useful, and young again. The job had become part of her; she truly believed that the Russian service could never find anyone more willing to work and to sacrifice herself when necessary. She knew, and the Okhrana bosses must know, that no male detective could replace her. They could tail the conspirators to the gates of their residences; she could follow them, if need be, into their bedrooms.

6. *(Continued)*

Paris Okhrana "Dissolved"

When these arguments proved of no avail, Mme. Le Davadie turned to Bittard-Monin with personal reproaches. No other agent he was dismissing had ever meant anything to him, while she had been his favorite before either of them had ever heard of the Okhrana. She recalled how she had shared with him her apartment and all in those young and idealistic years when he was struggling along as a poorly paid sub-inspector for the *Sûreté*. The ingrate would hear none of it; his heart had turned to stone. Aside from the change of policy, he reminded her coldly, the agents had to be dismissed for the obvious reason that they had all been blown by Burtzev and their names published in all the press of Europe, so they would be entirely useless.

"Why aren't you fired, then?" she came back. "Your name was not only in the newspapers, but proclaimed in parliament."

He said he would be, reiterating that the Okhrana was discontinuing operations and making a public announcement to that effect. He declared that part of the reason for this was to insure the safety of the agents whose names and addresses were now known to the terrorists. But he did not convince her. The argument degenerated into repetition and name-calling.

Finally Mme. Le Davadie saw that it was no use and signed the five papers. First was a receipt for 200 francs, her salary for the last month, and one for expense money and a termination bonus. Then there was the notarized resignation:

> The undersigned Madame Richard Le Davadie, residing at 52 rue Jacob, employed by the intelligence service organized and directed by Monsieur Marcel Bittard-Monin, am hereby resigning from said service as a result of its complete dissolution as of 31 October 1913.
>
> I have received as indemnity the sum of 200 francs, the equivalent of one month's salary.
>
> I declare that I am entirely satisfied with the payment of said sum as my final compensation.
>
> Paris, 31 October 1913
> Le Davadie G. Richard

Another paper acknowledged that she had been returned her birth certificate and a court document concerning herself. By her fifth subscription Mme. Le Davadie declared that she no longer had in her possession any notes, letters, ciphers, or photographs belonging to the service.

6. *(Continued)*

With the termination money in her purse and all the anger in her heart, Mme. Le Davadie went to the nearest bistro. She was a temperate woman and despised excessive drinking, but this time she had to have an outlet. Not from worry about her future but for her wrath toward Monin. She couldn't take her anger out on the faceless Okhrana. If she knew any of its officers, it would be different; but going to the Russian embassy without knowing anyone, as ex-agent Fontana once had done, would be futile and ridiculous. They would say they'd never heard of her or of Bittard-Monin or anyone like that.

Two other agents Monin had dismissed that day were in the bistro—Mme. Drouchot, whom Mme. Le Davadie knew well but disliked, and Auguste Pouchot, with whom she had once served on a surveillance team in Montreux. As an agent she would have never approached them publicly, but now, savoring her new freedom, she joined them at the table. No explanations were necessary; she saw at once that they both had been canned too. The three joined in cursing Bittard-Monin.

"The bastard should not have thrown *you* out," said Mme. Drouchot, meaningfully. Le Davadie felt like grabbing her hair for twisting this one in; then she realized that Mme. Drouchot had already taken more cognac than was needed to drown her bitterness. Pouchot too was nearly drunk. She determined at once not to follow their example. She had only one absinthe and sipped it slowly, thinking. Not really listening to the other two, she heard them naming Burtzev again and again, just as Monin had, it seemed a hundred times. Burtzev's revolutionary intelligence had busted Paris Okhrana. He was powerful, the Sherlock Holmes of the revolution. All the press of Paris was praising him, and the leading politicians were fighting his battles in parliament.

On the Victor's Bandwagon

Mme. Le Davadie made up her mind. Without even finishing her drink, she left her companions and went straight to the rue de La Glacière. She knew Burtzev's office well from having done surveillance on it. She would get even with Monin. She would join the revolutionary service; and Burtzev, now so strong and successful, would pay her just as he was paying Leroi, who had defected as Okhrana agent at about the time she had formally signed on in 1911. She would even be paid for her revenge.

6. *(Continued)*

The office at 53 rue de la Glacière was a noisier place than Monin's bureau. It was not large, but some half dozen people were engaged in heated discussions. Burtzev was not there; his assistant Leroi received her. This was well. She knew how much influence he had with Burtzev, and she thought he would help her. Back in 1908 he had been one of her more persistent admirers among the investigation agents. True that his awkwardly long figure, frequently unstable because of too much alcohol, had not attracted her even to the point of the camaraderie usual among fellow agents; but when he was sober and alone with her, he used to flatter her with attentions. Now he showed his surprise and joy at seeing her. He moved as though to kiss her in front of everyone but settled for kissing her hand. He took her to Burtzev's private office.

When the pleasantries were over, she described how she had quit Monin and the Okhrana, and much of what she said was quite untrue. They wanted her to stay, she said, but she was fed up with them all and wanted to get even, particularly with Monin and his net. She finally recognized, she said, that Burtzev was doing the right thing, and she would be glad to join him even at a small salary, just enough to keep her alive. She would help to the best of her ability to fight and expose the entire Russian service. Leroi was pleased, and they worked out a preliminary plan of employment that he thought would be acceptable to Burtzev. She also was pleased, and she forgot all her past antipathy for Leroi. He took her to dinner and she took him to her apartment.

The following day, on 1 November 1913, Mme. Richard Le Davadie was hired as agent of the revolutionary intelligence service. Leroi spoke enthusiastically to Burtzev about her exceptional qualities and vast knowledge of the personnel and activities of the Okhrana's non-Russian networks in France, Switzerland, and Italy, as well as her excellent current motivation. Burtzev was not opposed; but, seasoned as he was in the game and not sharing Leroi's personal reasons for enthusiasm, he wanted first to determine how much she knew and to make sure she was not a plant of some kind. She had to be interrogated in detail, be kept under surveillance for several days, and in the meantime be given no chance to learn anything about his service.

The first interrogation satisfied Burtzev about her knowledge, and the many questions about Okhrana targets, methods of surveillance, timing and location of operations, reporting procedures in clear and in code, and cooperation with local security organs convinced Le

68

6. *(Continued)*

Davadie that she was dealing with just as professional a service as the one she had left. She knew enough to fill a book, and since it would take forever to get this in debriefings, Burtzev told her to put in writing a full account of every surveillance job she had done since February 1911, when she formally became a salaried Okhrana agent. She could write this in the quiet of her own apartment.

Burtzev gave her 40 francs and the promise of a better monthly salary than that. All she had to do for the time being was write this report and keep in daily touch with Leroi or with Burtzev if Leroi was away. Leroi accompanied her home. Pleased as Punch, he wanted to celebrate right away, and on her 40 francs. But she was not in the mood. She was disturbed by his assurances of how they would have a secure job together and he would look after her, and especially by his remark that he personally would take care of the surveillance Burtzev wanted her kept under. She talked him out of coming up to her apartment this time.

Second Thoughts

Alone, it took her but little thinking to decide that she could never serve Leroi; that was about what this job would mean. And although Burtzev made a pleasant impression on her—the kindly, soft-spoken, bearded, scholarly gentleman knew how to treat a lady— those 40 francs of salary advance perturbed her. The appearance of the people in Burtzev's office, too, like Leroi's shabbiness, gave her shivers. They looked intellectual all right, but all haggard and undernourished. She understood no Russian, and their speaking it made her feel strange. No, she couldn't bring herself to associate with Leroi and those sallow-faced conspirators, even if the prospects of remuneration had been brighter than they were.

Late the same evening, after she had made up her mind not to go through with it, she had a visitor. Thinking it might be Leroi, she was not going to answer the door, but the knocking persisted and the caller spoke her last name. She opened to find Henri Bint there. She had met Bint on two occasions, but he had never been in her apartment. She liked the old reprobate. "Henri!" she called him by his first name as in the days when he organized her surveillance team. "I'm so pleased to see you. What a surprise!"

The call was not a social one. Bint said he was sorry about her dismissal from the Okhrana service but it was unavoidable for everyone, even for him after 35 years of service. She started talking about

6. *(Continued)*

the ingrates and was going to indulge in some more scolding, but Bint stopped her:

"You shouldn't feel bad.   You got yourself another job."
"What job?"   She looked puzzled.
"With Burtzev's service.   I know it all."

How could Bint, a mortal enemy of Leroi, know?   He knew just when she had made the two visits to Burtzev's office, what she had said to Leroi and Burtzev, what they said to her, and what was decided.   He even knew about the 40 francs and her assignment to write about the Okhrana.   He did not tell her that Jollivet, another "dismissed" Okhrana agent whom Mme. Le Davadie had never known, had recently been employed by Burtzev and had been in the office both times.

Mme. Le Davadie was not at all embarrassed.   She told Bint she had just decided not to work for Burtzev after all.   But Bint had a different idea, and that was the reason for his visit.   He had a simple plan: she should not only go ahead with Burtzev but perform so well as to make herself indispensable in the office on the rue de la Glacière.   She needed persuading.   They talked until after midnight.   She warned him that Leroi might come around, for she was to be under his surveillance for some time.   Bint knew all that; he had disposed of Leroi by seeing to it that he had a drinking partner at a cabaret.

Le Davadie insisted that under no circumstances would she ever work again with Bittard-Monin.

"Of course not," Bint said.   "Your position will be completely changed.   You will no longer be a detective conducting surveillance and investigating through local security offices.   That is a thing of the past for you.   You will no longer be an overt agent for anyone.   Your position will be that of a secret agent reporting to the Okhrana the inside story of revolutionary espionage and propaganda."   She liked the secrecy and the adventurousness of the proposal.   "But it would be dangerous!   To whom would I be reporting?   You?"

"Maybe to me at times, but the Russians prefer to handle the secret agents themselves.   All important dealings would be with them."

"How much will they pay?"

Bint did not know exactly, but he was sure that as secret agent she would be getting much higher pay than ever before, depending partly upon herself.   As for the dangers, he said that the Okhrana people knew how to play it safe; she would only have to follow their

70

6. *(Continued)*

instructions. He told her he would visit her once more and then arrange a meeting with a Russian for further instructions. He promised to help her write the long story of her agent career that Burtzev required.

Leroi, showing the signs of his night of drinking, called in the middle of the afternoon. He found her at the table, in cheerful spirits, writing her report. He went on to the office to tell Burtzev that he had had the new recruit under surveillance and that she was now at home doing the required writing.

On 4 November Le Davadie went to Burtzev's office again. She brought a sheaf of papers in her own handwriting, done hastily and without much concern for tidiness. They listed in simple chronological order, from 15 February 1911 to 29 October 1913, her singleton and team assignments—dates, locations, targets, where and how picked up, whom with, where followed. In several instances the assistance of local security organs was noted. The story was impressive in the quantity of data recalled but not so elaborate as to suggest reference to contemporary records. It had of course been prepared by Bint, from the records in Bittard-Monin's office. Before giving it to Le Davadie to copy he had also consulted Sushkov, assistant to Krassilnikov.

New Jane at Work

It is not known what code name Burtzev gave Le Davadie, who now became an operative in the revolutionary service. Krassilnikov and all the Okhrana office thenceforth referred to her as Jane. A great pile of reports from December 1913 to late summer 1914, when Burtzev folded up his office and returned to Russia, attests that she knew and reported every move made by the revolutionaries. The records indicate that all her reports were in writing, urgent ones in the convenient *enveloppes pneumatiques* which were handled like telegrams, others in ordinary registered mail, often addressed to Bint's cover firm. At no time, it appears, did she arouse suspicion in Burtzev or his staff.

She reported first on several French and Italian agents Monin had dismissed who came to Burtzev in search of employment. In an effort to ingratiate themselves, these would all disparage Le Davadie's reputation as a person or an agent. A Mme. Tiercelin, in particular, made vitriolic attacks on her as Monin's and other agents' mistress; but Burtzev and Leroi did not care. Le Davadie did not hide any-

6. *(Continued)*

thing—like that—from them, and she proved to be a good agent. They never suspected that all her reporting to them actually came from 79 rue de la Grenelle or was at least approved there.

Thanks to Jane, the Okhrana was able to forstall a number of terrorist attempts during this period. It was she who led Krassilnikov onto the trail of a certain Bessel as he left Brindisi for Macedonia to pick up a load of bombs for assassins in Russia. He was arrested in Belgrade and his shipment confiscated on a train in Serbia. By a curious coincidence, Jane was also assigned to help Burtzev prepare evidence of Bessel's innocence for the revolutionary press to use in showing that the charges for the arrest in Belgrade had been trumped up by the Okhrana.

Jane reported on the speeches Burtzev prepared for Jaurez to deliver in the French parliament attacking the Okhrana. In some instances the Okhrana thus had Jaurez's speeches before he himself had seen them. During the first half of 1914, when Burtzev exposed a considerable bag of Okhrana agents, both Russian and non-Russian, Jane could at least warn when and how they would be exposed. She became so important to Burtzev that he wanted to take her with him early in 1914 on a campaign to expose the activities of the Russian secret service in the Italian parliament. She consulted Krassilnikov, who actually approved the trip, but she preferred to develop an acute migrane: she was afraid that it might bring to light discrepancies in her first report to Burtzev with respect to cooperation with Italian security personnel.

It is evident from Okhrana records that Jane ceased to be an agent after Burtzev's departure and the closing of his service. She apparently located some war-related employment; in August and September 1914 at least half the personnel of the Okhrana abroad were drafted into military services.

Soon after the outbreak of the revolution a number of writers began competing in their efforts to expose all Okhrana secret agents. Jane's role was somehow never exposed, even by writer Agafonov, who as a member of the commission investigating the Okhrana had full access to her papers. It is possible that he was unable to detect her identity behind the cover name. Several writers named Le Davadie among the non-Russian investigation agents belonging to the Bittard-Monin network, but all ignore not only her services for Burtzev but her double role for the Okhrana.

72

La Petite

Three intelligence services used "the little one"—the revolutionaries when she was a child, the Austrians against Russia, and the Russians against Austria.   The files of Paris Okhrana contained only 3 x 5 cards on the activities of her parents, but Pavel Zavarzin, Warsaw Okhrana chief at the time of the childhood episode, has told her story.

Living Doll

The Warsaw Okhrana office was located in the Hôtel de Ville, a large building which also provided living quarters for Zavarzin and his subordinates with their families. Beginning in 1904, milk was delivered in a large can to the Zavarzin apartment by an eleven-year-old girl.   It came from a dairy where her mother was also employed. The girl was diminutive and charming.   She had light, fluffy blond hair and brilliant blue eyes, like a doll.   Everybody called her La Petite.   Pleased by her promptness and friendliness, the occupants of the Hôtel de Ville spoiled her with gifts of all sorts.   A particular attachment was formed between her and the children of Yan, Zavarzin's coachman.

This pleasant association flourished for two years.   Then one day a surveillance team was tailing a female terrorist named Rotte.   She was accompanied by a young girl carrying a milk can, apparently full.   They both went into a house in the Warsaw suburb Praga; within five minutes the girl came out alone and without the can. The detectives now recognized her as La Petite.   One of them followed to see where she would go next.   Surveilling a child proved to be a difficult game: she often stopped and played at corners or wandered down side streets looking in the windows.   After two hours she was back at home.

A penetration of a terrorist group reported at about this time that groups preparing assassinations and robberies were using children to deliver arms, one piece at a time, to the perpetrators.   A child carrying a package or container with a small gun or bomb inside would be followed by a terrorist at some distance, then overtaken at the place of action.   The investigation of a number of terrorist acts confirmed that this was indeed the practice.   Penetrations reported also that the conspirators maintained surveillance of the Okhrana premises in a way that would never be detected.   The conspirators knew the tag numbers of Okhrana carriages and the names of officers

6. *(Continued)*

and surveillance agents. Still another report said that the subversives had possession of some important documents stolen from the Okhrana office.

Elaborate security precautions had always been taken to keep unauthorized personnel off the Okhrana premises. La Petite was the only outsider ever admitted to the official quarters, and now she had been seen with the terrorist Rotte. A few forgotten incidents of the past two years were now recalled. One morning, Zavarzin himself remembered, he had found Yan's wife and daughter Handzhia cleaning his office, and La Petite was with them. When he asked what she was doing there, "After I delivered the milk I came to see Handzhia," she had said.

She spoke perfect Russian. Her explanation was that her father, although a Pole from Austria, spoke only Russian at home, having learned it during years of employment in a Moscow brewery. After his death three years earlier her mother had come to work in Warsaw.

Zavarzin recalled also that one morning his administrative assistant was unable to find a batch of papers which he thought he had—carelessly—left on a table the night before. A thorough search was made without success. Moreover, La Petite was often seen in the carriage shed and the dressing room where agents changed into coachman's uniform for surveillance assignments.

La Petite and her mother were both placed under surveillance. It was soon learned that the woman lived with Mishas, an influential member of the Polish Socialist Party, and that this man had been accompanied by La Petite on walks through the city. It was decided that the mother, being an Austrian subject, should be expelled from Warsaw and should be induced to take La Petite with her.

Zavarzin had them both brought to his office. The mother, named Kusitska, was cooperative but evasive when it came to giving information. When she realized he knew about her daughter's activity, she admitted through tears that she had been unable to counteract the corrupting pressure of the revolutionaries upon her child. She would therefore be glad to leave Warsaw for any place where she could get the girl away from their vicious influence and enroll her in some school.

"One would not give her ten years," she said, "and she's already thirteen. She did spy on your office at first, but after being treated so kindly by you all she was ashamed and stopped. Didn't you?"

The girl was all red in the face, too embarrassed to answer, or more likely unwilling to confirm a patent lie.

6. *(Continued)*

Reunion

Nine years later, when Russia and Austria were at war and Zavarzin was in charge of the Okhrana office in Odessa, he received a telephone call late in the evening. A woman's voice: "Hello, Colonel Zavarzin, Chief of Section." No one ever addressed him thus by title. Whose was this strange, attractive voice?

"I must see you urgently, but not in your office. I'm calling from the railroad station. Tell me a good hotel where we can meet."

"But who are you?"

"La Petite from Warsaw. Do you remember me?"

She stayed in the Hotel London, but the meeting took place in a safe house. Zavarzin instructed Budakov, his chief of surveillance, to arrange for complete coverage after the meeting. He did not share Budakov's fears for the meeting itself—that La Petite might come with a pistol in her muff.

She came in, still small for a grown woman, scintillating with pleasure: "You remember me! That's so wonderful! But I'm no longer the subversive La Petite of Warsaw. I have become your ally. Before coming in I asked this man [Budakov] to inspect my bag. One could of course expect anything from La Petite of the past." Zavarzin soon realized that she had become a professional intelligence agent. But whose?

"You have no doubt taken measures to keep me under surveillance," she plunged in. "That's important, because at one after midnight tonight I am to meet at the Variété a man I don't know. I'm to be introduced to him by a woman who is appearing in the show as a famous sharpshooter. The man is in touch with the Austrian general staff, and it will be important for you to keep him under close watch. He is one of the top Austrian agents here. Then tomorrow I am going to Petersburg to see Okhrana chief Bieletzky, who will probably take me to the imperial general staff. It may be that on the road to Petersburg I shall be met by persons in whom you may be interested, so you will probably want to have me covered all the way through."

Having disposed of this urgent matter on her mind, the attractive visitor proposed dinner. She was tired and hungry; the wartime trip from Vienna to Odessa was by no means without hardships. After the meal she was ready to talk about her past. But first she wanted to thank Zavarzin as the great benefactor who had played an important role in her life. Instead of putting her mother and her in prison

6. *(Continued)*

he had given them good advice and sent them to safety. Her mother, La Petite said, had been a weak woman; for a little love she had become a slave to Mishas. His every word came to be an order for both mother and child. La Petite delivered dynamite and bombs for the Rotte woman and other terrorists. It was Mishas' plan to blow up the Warsaw Okhrana office and kill Zavarzin. As a child she had been fascinated by the plan, and Mishas became a hero in her eyes. Three years after leaving Warsaw, when she read in the newspapers about the apprehension of the Warsaw terrorists, including Mishas, and their trial and execution, she realized how criminal her activities had been.

Zavarzin probably did not swallow whole the story of her remorse, for he changed the conversation with a question about the color of her hair. As a child it was light blond, now nearly jet black. How come? She said she dyed it in order to look older. Then she went back to what had happened since she last saw him at thirteen.

Tale of Two Services

Upon arrival in Lvov her mother sent her to a convent for schooling and to learn dressmaking. It was a harsh life, with constant work or kneeling in prayer and frequent cruel punishment as she grew rebellious. More often than not she was hungry, and after her mother's death she had no affection from anyone. One day the mother superior found her crying in the cold chapel, took pity on her, and promised thereafter to be a mother to her. Life remained hard, but under the old abbess' protection Seraphine, as she was named in the convent, became an obedient pupil.

After six years of convent life she was employed in the household of a wealthy Galician merchant. A romance soon developed with the merchant's nephew and they were married. He was a panslavist employed by the Russian services, and thus both newly-weds were soon working for the Russians in Austrian Galicia.

When the war broke out the Austrians drafted her husband, and soon thereafter he was taken prisoner by the Russians. La Petite, after giving birth to a child, made up her mind to get to Russia at all costs. She thought of the possibility of being taken into the Austrian espionage service and sent there. Leaving the baby with her mother-in-law, she set up as a dressmaker catering to various families of army officers. In time she found an officer of the general staff who was interested in more than her dressmaking.

6. *(Continued)*

Her frequent night meetings with this man gave her a chance to let him see her, incidentally, as an Austrian patriot who knew Warsaw extremely well, spoke Russian perfectly, and was intelligent and resourceful. She did not need to prompt him to the proposal that she would do well in Austrian intelligence. With all the modesty Seraphine had learned in the convent, she replied that she had no experience to fit her for such work, but he insisted that she should at least give it a try. After a few days of thinking it over, she decided that there would be nothing wrong in tentative acceptance.

They tried all sorts of tests on her. Questions were shot at her in the least expected forms. She would be left alone in an office with documents marked secret scattered on the desks and watched through a peephole to see whether she showed undue interest in the papers. She was followed on city streets to determine whether she had assimilated the psychological training they had given her in operational conduct and patriotism. After two months' training the Austrians set up an interview with a German officer. He interrogated her in German and Russian and found her Russian more fluent than her German. When he learned that the convent had given her considerable training in caring for the sick, he named her on the spot chief nurse in a hospital for seriously wounded Russian prisoners. It was he who insisted that she dye her hair black so as to look old enough to be a chief nurse. Her job was to attend the wounded and report anything they might say, perhaps in delirium, of interest to the German forces.

After three months of this service, she was summoned before a captain and told she had been assigned an important mission on which much would be expected of her.

"From now on your name shall be Anna Yakovlevna Lyubova, with Tyumen in Siberia as your place of origin. Here is your passport. It is a genuine document: the real Lyubova is here in Austria. She is married and has no desire to return to Russia. You will take her place among a large group of Russians who are being repatriated in exchange for Austrians from Russia. In this assignment you will have to exercise much prudence, and if there are difficulties you will have to be guided by your patriotism. We all put our country first . . ."

The entire operational program, with many alternative courses of action, was outlined for "Lyubova." She was to contact Austrian agents and deliver them instructions all along the way, as far as

6. *(Continued)*

Vladivostok. From there she was to go on to Harbin and then proceed to Shanghai, where she should report to the German consulate.

L'Autrichienne

From Odessa Zavarzin promptly wired to Petersburg headquarters the whole long story. Surveilling La Petite and her German contacts the same night, Budakov found that the introduction and meeting took place as she had told. The sharpshooter woman and the German man, named Gross, were both exiled to Siberia for the duration; there was not enough proof to hang them.

La Petite revealed also that the German dreadnoughts "Goeben" and "Breslau" were heading for the Black Sea to bombard Russian ports. This information was confirmed within a few days. Although Zavarzin had reported the intelligence promptly, the defense command was in no position to take counter action, and the attack caused havoc in several harbors.

"Lyubova" was carefully watched on her way to Petersburg, where she went directly to the Okhrana chief as scheduled. He had her case transferred to military intelligence, and there was no trace in Okhrana files of her subsequent whereabouts and activities. Years after his exile, Zavarzin speculated that a dashing young lady of her description who lived in Monte Carlo and was known as "l'Autrichienne," speaking perfect Russian and Polish, of angelic beauty, and wildly spending her Brazilian husband's wealth, could be La Petite.

Miscellaneous

THE YOUNG STALIN. By *Edward Ellis Smith.* (New York: Farrar, Straus, and Giroux. 1967. 470 pp. $8.50.)

This book is built around the thesis that Stalin was an Okhrana agent throughout his prerevolutionary career, and all the evidence presented—the product of a very substantial research effort—is shaped to fit this view. The results are sometimes persuasive but frequently awkward and incredible, even to a reader who was originally predisposed toward the author's thesis.

For Mr. Smith tries too hard. All too often, when evidence is either lacking or completely ambiguous, he constructs a highly speculative and improbable hypothesis which he later alludes to as established fact. (His depiction of Stalin's supposed conspiratorial relationship in 1913 with the Bolshevik leader and known Okhrana agent Ramon Malinovsky—at a time when by Smith's own showing Stalin was in very bad odor with the Okhrana—is an example of such a hypothesis.) More than once he sets forth an impressive generalization which he himself subsequently undermines, apparently unwittingly: thus he attaches (p. 59) tremendous sinister significance to the fact that Stalin "alone" escaped arrest in the Okhrana raids in Tiflis in March 1901 but three pages later alludes in passing to a more important Georgian revolutionary, Ketskhoveli, who had similarly escaped. This overenthusiastic approach to the facts creates unnecessary distrust in the reader and weakens confidence in some conclusions which may nevertheless be correct.

The author does best in the first third of his narrative: although he does not *prove* his thesis, there seems nothing inherently impossible and much that is reasonable in his suggestion that Dzhugashvili may have been tapped by the Okhrana as a low-level agent shortly after his expulsion from the Tiflis seminary in 1899, that he systematically informed on comrades in party organizations in Tiflis, Baku, and Batum over the next few years, that he acquired a highly unsavory reputation among the Social Democrats of each city in turn, that he was finally arrested for cover purposes in 1902 when revolutionary suspicions about him were about to boil over, and that the Okhrana furnished

104

7. *(Continued)*

the otherwise invisible means of support for the family he acquired after 1904.

It is after this that Smith begins increasingly to strain the evidence. He insists that the Okhrana was behind Stalin's masterminding of the particularly bloody and ill-fated Yerevan Square robbery in Tiflis in June 1907, although he is not consistent enough even to examine the question of whether the Okhrana endorsed all the other Caucasus "expropriations" Stalin is believed to have planned for the Bolsheviks in 1906 and 1907. These operations were congenial work for Stalin, and it was through them that he first acquired importance in Lenin's eyes—surely sufficient motivation in itself for performing them. From here on the effort to explain Stalin's behavior in terms of supposed Okhrana operations becomes ludicrous in the light of what both the Okhrana and Stalin actually did. The Okhrana arrested Stalin five times in the nine years between March 1908 and the February Revolution, and it left him at large a total of 3 months in 1908, 6 months in 1909, 3 months in 1910, 2 months in 1911, 6 months in 1912, 2 months in 1913, and not at all in 1914, 1915, or 1916. In September 1911 Stalin had barely been in St. Petersburg two days before he was picked up again and sent back to his term in exile. This seems to go well beyond any conceivable requirements of cover. For Stalin's part, when he was helping to run *Pravda* in St. Petersburg late in 1912 he took a temporarily conciliatory line toward the Mensheviks—which, as Smith admits, was precisely the opposite of what was wanted by both the Okhrana and Lenin.

Smith recognizes that Stalin was not at all under Okhrana control by 1912, yet stubbornly insists (p. 202) that he must have continued to have a regular contact in the Department of Police in St. Petersburg to whom he supposedly could plan to denounce Roman Malinovsky for disloyalty to the Okhrana. One of the weakest aspects of the book is the failure to consider carefully when such links must have disappeared, at what point Stalin must have decided to opt for the Bolsheviks rather than the police. The evidence provided in the book itself suggests strongly that this occurred much earlier than the author is willing to admit, and that if Stalin had once had a foot in the Okhrana camp it was probably withdrawn by 1907 or 1908.

Harry Gelman

7. *(Continued)*

Agent Stalin

Dear Sirs:

I should like to comment a little further on *The Young Stalin*, by Edward Ellis Smith, which you recently reviewed.[1] I agree with your reviewer that the author tries too hard to show that Stalin was an agent of the Tsarist Okhrana and that he remained one over too many years, but I do not find the evidence very persuasive even for the early period.

Part of the case for the agent thesis rests upon the portrayal of Stalin as a daring revolutionary hero prominent in organizing strikes, writing proclamations, setting up underground printshops, and inciting the populace to rebellion; how could he be doing all this and yet moving about almost with impunity in the Caucasus if he were not in collusion with the police? But this picture of the young Stalin derives from Soviet writers in the period of his dictatorship who had no choice but to depict him with panegyrics. Biographers who did not have to cater to Stalin's glorification—from Trotsky down to revolutionary Georgians in exile—speak of him (under his nicknames Soso, Koba, etc.) as an unimportant little malcontent, unnoticed not only by the police but by the early revolutionaries. He had little reason to hide.

Then there are the documents in the files of the Paris Okhrana, preserved at the Hoover Institution, which Smith tries to use in support of his theory but which really point in the opposite direction. Okhrana

---

[1] *Studies* XII 1, p. 104 f.

120

7. *(Continued)*

headquarters sent the Paris office Stalin's name and description as a subversive or suspect on four occasions between 1904 and 1911; these are the only references to him in the files. Now the Petersburg headquarters would not have informed Paris about the identity of agents working for it at home, within the Empire; but when a revolutionary was recruited as an agent his name was as a rule deleted from the roster of subversives, and Headquarters circulated to all outposts lists of names to be deleted without giving any reason therefor. Stalin's name appears on no such circular.

Moreover, it was Headquarters' practice to inform Paris, as well as all outposts at home, about people who had in any way served as agents or informers but then either were dropped as unreliable or deserted the service of their own volition. If Stalin had been an informer or penetration agent and dropped out in 1912 when opted by Lenin for the Central Committee, the Okhrana home office which had controlled him would have prepared such a circular for dissemination to the outposts. There is no such circular on Stalin. Even if he had served the Okhrana only in the very first years of his adult life, as a student at the Theological Seminary or employee at the Tiflis Geophysical Observatory, when he was dismissed he would have been reported in the circulars as a defector or an informer "not meriting confidence" (*nezasluzhivayushchi doveria*); scores of such circulars were disseminated regularly. But his name is not included in any of them.

If Stalin had been informing some local police agent on fellow students in the Seminary, he would most likely have been forced to continue. Instead of letting him be expelled as a student and fired as an employee, each time against his own wishes, the Okhrana would have seen to it that the Seminary retained him, just as it did other agents among the students. Smith himself cites the case of agent Demetrashili, who began his career at the same Theological Seminary in Tiflis; he was made to continue with his schooling and eventually converted into a regular penetration agent. The same Folder No. 1 at the Hoover Institution on Deep Cover Agents which documents this case shows that again and again students and government employees were reinstated or re-hired at the request of the police organs.

Incidentally, in referring to the Okhrana structure and personnel strength, Mr. Smith makes without documentation statements that are completely unrealistic. For example, he credits the Okhrana with having in Petersburg, when Stalin came there in 1909, 2,500 profes-

7. *(Continued)*

sional intelligence officers. According to all official tabulations, the entire Okhrana at home and abroad could not muster a staff of that size. Smith also questions Stalin's access to documentation and funds. But most of the revolutionaries had the same problem, and quite a few of them moved around much more than Stalin. Especially for the Social Democrats, documentation was somehow always abundant. Mr. Smith could have found at the Hoover Institute scores of listings of all types of passports used by the Bolsheviks—of their own manufacture, stolen, doctored, or obtained officially through penetration.

Despite its forced inferences about Stalin as agent, *The Young Stalin* has value in documenting the dictator's character as manifested in its formative stages. He is similarly described in a perhaps still unpublished manuscript to be found in Trotsky's files:

> His youthful companions characterized him as sullen and quite unlike his comrades in the nature of his activities. Wherever he appeared in his revolutionary travels, there was talk of intrigue, breakdown of discipline, arbitrary behavior, slander of comrades, and denouncing of opponents to the police. Many of these reports were probably based on lies, but no other revolutionary gave rise to talk of such a nature . . . Koba's name never appeared in any of our correspondence. He considered that, being a provincial, he was slow getting ahead, and he looked on others with envy.

Rita T. Kronenbitter

Lightning Source UK Ltd.
Milton Keynes UK
UKOW021956250612

195022UK00004B/2/P